BELOVED

A Widow's Journey

Carol Irace-Brunetti

ISBN 978-1-64458-963-2 (paperback)
ISBN 978-1-64458-964-9 (digital)

Christian Faith Publishing, Inc.
832 Park Avenue
Meadville, PA 16335
www.christianfaithpublishing.com

Printed in the United States of America

Chapter 1

It is a beautiful, warm summer afternoon where the sun is hot, and the sky is a beautiful dark blue as is usual for this time of year in Rhode Island. Birds of all kinds: doves, chickadees, nut hatches, gold finches, and cardinals fly over our porch because they are headed for the bird feeders on the edge of the woods where we feed them. Life is good as I am healing from my double knee-replacement surgery that I had four weeks ago. I am spending this time sitting on the porch, relaxing and enjoying the warm sunshine as I cannot do much else. All I keep thinking about is I can't wait to get moving again to work in my garden and be able to walk in the grass and enjoy our beautiful yard.

Robert, my husband, is such a fanatic about our lawn, it is plush and green like a well-manicured carpet. We have friends that call it his kingdom, and every summer, they will come over and kneel in front of it. It is quite hilarious. He spends time mowing it, watering it, and caring for it, and if he needed to, he would use scissors to manicure it. I am sure you are getting the point. If a dandelion dares to appear on our lawn, it is sorry. He takes a long screwdriver and digs it out. Every night, as he drives up our long 750' driveway from work, he looks for yellow to see if another one dared to appear. When our kids were younger about twelve to thirteen years old, he would have them mow it with a push mower. My kids would complain, "Why do we have to push the lawn when we have a riding lawn mower in the shed?" He told them because he likes to look at the grass with straight lines in it to give the appearance of a ballpark. As the kids are older now and have jobs of their own, he enjoys mowing it at least twice a week himself and smiles as he is doing it. My kids and I have named the lawn mower "his mistress" because he spends so much time with it. We all get a good laugh from that.

The flower beds and gardens are my specialty. I love planting beautiful flowers, roses, herbs, and shrubs that accent our yard and make the colors come alive. Every year, I plant many flats of flowers that our yard looks like a park when they are all in full bloom. I strategically plant flowers for every season in every bed so there is color from spring until fall. I often find myself weeding and fluffing the mulch in the flower beds to give them a nice clean look, that is after Robert would have to edge the lawn and the cuttings go into my garden.

So here I am, sitting on our back porch, looking out over the beautifully-manicured green lawn and flower beds in full bloom that I had planted before my surgery as we have an agreement. He takes care of the lawn, and I take care of the flower beds. Together, they accent each other beautifully. For the last four weeks, he has had to do both as I am unable to walk across the lawn by myself.

He is so thoughtful, after a long day at work, he comes home and takes me for a walk where he holds both of my hands and walks backward as I am beginning to learn to walk with my new knees. I am a little unstable on the grass as it is a softer surface than the hardwood floors on the inside of our home. We do everything together and enjoy each other's company so much that he is trying to help me recover as quickly as I can. He has been cooking the meals and waiting on me hand and foot. He even slept in the hospital for three nights with me and then got up and went to work each morning. He wanted to make sure that I was taken good care of by the nurses and the hospital staff. He is always concerned for me, wants to protect me and take of me. That's just the kind of husband he is.

As I sat there that warm July day and life was good, my knees were healing and finally, for once, I didn't have to crawl up the stairs in pain to go to bed. Robert began complaining about a pain in his back, so I told him to go to the doctor, which he did after work that day. We had just finished a large reconstruction project at our church where he picked up a heavy piece of machinery by himself and he had hurt his back.

What the doctor discovers is not what we could have ever imagined. As he came home from the doctor's office, he found me on the back porch where I was sitting. I could tell instantly that something was very wrong before he even began to tell me all what the doctor had to say. He has lung cancer. We just sat there together arm in arm, hugging and crying, crying and hugging. Neither of us could believe the diagnosis. You hear of these things happening to other people but never to you or your family. All he could say was, "I have just been handed a death sentence."

We knew he needed prayer, so we called our family, our pastor, and our closest friends. That evening, our pastor came to our home and prayed with us. He made a commitment to us that we would walk this journey together. He was deeply saddened by the news as he was not only our pastor but a good friend. It is during these difficult times that you need to know there is someone you can lean on and know they will be there for you. Robert, as a husband, father, and provider needed to know that all will be taken care of in case something happened. Our pastor was that reassurance we needed.

So as the days pass by, Robert has to go for a series of tests at the hospital, and after we sought out several opinions, it is confirmed—he has stage 4 lung cancer and has only two to four months to live. At fifty-five years of age, we never thought we would hear that diagnosis as both of his parents are in their eighties, enjoying good health. We have been married for thirty-four years and have three beautiful children, a daughter and two sons, we are so in love and have been best friends for the past thirty-seven years, life was good. How could this happen to us?

That day, our life changed forever!

As I am walking this journey, I am asking that you read along with an open heart and mind and allow me to tell you my story. I pray in some way my journey will bless you, help you, encourage you, direct you, lead you and give you hope.

Chapter 2

Cancer is a word that I can't stand saying or hearing, and I would love to withdraw it from the English language.

Robert's lung was full of fluid and had to be drained every day. His cancer was the size of a peanut and had positioned itself in the one spot that was inoperable, between the lung and the lung lining. Because it was there, his lung filled with the fluid that surrounded his lung, and he had to have a port put in that the visiting nurse came to drain. Because of the fluid, it was hard for him to breathe and could no longer work, although he tried for a couple of weeks.

After we swallowed the disturbing news of his diagnosis, we began the process of doctors, second opinion, third opinion, and a load of tests in the hospital. They all gave the same diagnosis, he has only two to four months to live. If he chooses to do chemotherapy, his life may be extended a few more months.

As we sat in the oncologist's office on the day of our consultation, we listened as he explained the diagnosis to us, and he held back no punches. It felt like someone was kicking me in the stomach and in my heart at the same time. He began to explain what is about to happen to his body and what the future holds along with options in regard to treatments that we had to begin immediately. Sitting there in the oncologist's office, both of us appear strong as we have the opportunity to ask all the questions that we have, but we are unable to speak. I could physically feel my back become stiff like a board as I was trying not to begin bawling like a baby. I kept telling myself that I had to remain strong for him, but also, I need to absorb all the information that the doctor was explaining to us.

After our consultation with the doctor and his associate is over, we walked through the door to the outside of the building and stood on the sidewalk. There we looked at each other with complete unbelief as we both broke down. We grabbed a hold of each other and held tight as we were both sobbing uncontrollably. People were walking by us and obviously knew that we had just gotten some bad news as we are standing in front of the oncologist's office.

Robert, myself, our kids, family, friends, church, and everyone we know was praying for a healing from the Lord, and we believed that Jesus would heal his body. Robert's best friend had mentioned to us about a church that has a healing ministry, so we had visited there a few times to receive prayer. Robert and I both had gone to the altar for prayer. I personally have struggled with RLS, Restless Leg Syndrome, for many years where I can't sit down at night without my legs feeling like they are crawling and jumping. I would pace the floor every night to get the blood flowing in my legs as sleep was very difficult for me with RLS. I would hang my legs over the side of the bed during the night to keep the blood flowing. This particular church where we have gone to visit for a healing for him, I received a healing in my legs. Praise the Lord! The pastor has also been very supportive and has even come to our house to pray for Robert.

We began our journey with the Lord in April 1986, when we gave Jesus our lives and our hearts. We have served Him as youth pastors, board members, heads of ministries, and pre-marriage counselors. We have walked with the Lord for over thirty years and have been faithful, so we believed that of course, God would heal him. We believed that we would have an amazing testimony because of this illness, and one day, he would be preaching again and giving the glory to God for his healing.

Robert is a man's man, he is rough, tough, and his body is very muscular. As a union electrician, he travels from job to job and has met hundreds of men. His reputation amongst the trades for being the arm wrestling champion, is a testament to his strength. To this day, no one has ever beat him though many have tried.

His personality may seem rough and tough. but he has a way about him that his very presence demands respect from those around him. If he has something to say, he was going to say it, and you are going to listen. He was determined to be true to himself and not let anyone try to change who he was. He said, "God gave me this personality for a reason, so no one can ever push anything over on me."

I have heard stories from men he works with that say when they were in apprenticeship school together, everyone would try to sit next to him because he was such a likable guy and was hilarious with his very funny sarcastic one-liners. One night, at our dining room table during dinner, he tells me and the kids that he was going to fast from his sarcasm because he felt that he was too sarcastic. He was. Well, let me say that the fast only lasted about forty-five minutes. He couldn't stop. I told him that is how God made him so just enjoy it but be careful what you say.

He was very aware of his strengths and weaknesses and what was going on around him. As well as knowing that he was a leader and in control of every situation he found himself in. For the first time in his life, he couldn't control the outcome, he couldn't control the cancer, he couldn't just believe a healing into being.

We both knew that "time" is what we needed. To be together longer and enjoy many more years as we grow older. In time, scientists may discover the cure for lung cancer so the decision to begin chemotherapy was made. The first day of chemotherapy is long. but he feels fine and feels confident that he could do this, he could handle the strong dose of chemo they were giving him. On the following day, we returned to receive the injection of white blood cells and hydration.

By day three, a spiral of events has overtaken him. He began to hallucinate as the poison of chemotherapy began to spread through his body trying to fight against the cancer. He couldn't sleep, and this continued for ten consecutive days. He began to see things that are not there and even argued with us that we are wrong because we couldn't see what he saw, but he believed he was truly seeing them. He was hallucinating.

As he sat in a chair in our living room, he would look out through the set of French doors that overlooked our backyard. As he was looking outside, he was convinced that there was a man with a red hat on hiding behind our above ground pool. As he was obviously troubled by the thought of a man hiding in our backyard, I went outside and checked behind the pool; my daughter, Moriah, went outside and checked behind the pool, but he would not believe us that no one was there. That afternoon, his brother came over to visit, and he told him about the man and had him go and check behind the pool but there was no man. It was a red leaf that was hanging from a tree next to the pool, and he thought it was a red hat. His hallucinations are both funny and sad—heart-wrenching actually.

Another day, Robert was getting upset because as an electrician, he had a work van with all his tools and some equipment inside the van, he told us that someone stole his van. That he heard someone come and break in and drive it away. We told him that he was mistaken, but he became mad with us and told us we were lying to him. My son, Corey, had to go outside and take a picture of it to show him that the van was still in the driveway.

My heart was broken as I began to see my strong husband being brought to such lows. I know it was the chemotherapy doing this to his mind as well as lack of sleep. Whenever he tried to nap, his body would jump and jolt as his arms and legs would fly out from his body. Friends and family stopped by to visit and was shocked at what his body was doing and how it was reacting to this so-called medicine. At times, when he did nap, he would pretend to be drinking coffee or using his screw driver with the actions of his hands and arms. As funny as it was to watch, my heart was tearing into pieces.

One afternoon, as we were sitting there in the living room, he told me that his mind was going into some dark places. I instantly knew what he meant as I knew him that well. I told my son to hide my husband's gun as I was fearful that he may decide to use it.

Day nine, he was on the bathroom floor all curled up like a baby, feeling like he was ready to vomit.

Day ten, he finally fell asleep and slept for almost twenty-four hours straight, and in such a deep sleep that nothing would wake him up.

Day eleven, he woke up normal and back to himself again.

Wow, what a ride that was!!

Round two of chemotherapy is scheduled to begin in two days. We have a decision to make.

Together, we sit on the side of our bed and talk about this decision to continue or not. I know that he has already made up his mind, but I am listening to him as he is the one going through it, but together, we came up with the decision. Like I said, he likes to be in control but feels this needs to be a joint decision because both of us will be affected. We can definitely see that chemotherapy isn't an option any longer as it only brought darkness and poison into his body. He also told me that he thought about suicide, and I told him about moving the gun, and he said that was a wise move.

Not going back for another round is our decision—no more chemotherapy. We are sitting there on the side of our bed and begin to pray together as we have decided to leave his life in the Lord's hands! We choose our faith in Jesus! Robert has put his life—his physical body—in God's care.

We have faith that if God wants him alive, then no matter what happens, He will heal him, but if this is his journey's end, then so be it. We had given our lives to the Lord in 1986, over thirty years ago, and we have served Him in life, and if Robert's death is God's will, then he will serve Him in death. If God has chosen that this is his time to die, then who are we to fight it.

We prayed every day and believed for a miracle. God knows we needed one.

Robert cried often, and says, "Why not me, why not me?" as we were praying, He meant why couldn't he be one that God chose to heal. Daily, we read our Bibles, prayed, and worshiped together. I had no answers for him when he would ask those questions. My heart was being torn in so many little pieces as I saw this man that I have shared my life with being brought to this point.

Just believing something will happen doesn't mean that it is God's will for your life.

As little girls, we were taught about fairy tales and princesses. We met when I was sixteen years old and got married at nineteen, and he was twenty-one. I always felt we were living out my fairy tale. We served and loved the Lord. We had three beautiful children, a beautiful home, and we loved each other so much that we often felt we didn't need anyone else. We were truly happy. We were best friends and had a wonderful marriage. We were blessed!

So this here, him having cancer, this was definitely not part of our plan.

Chapter 3

News, news, news. The news is always on, the local news, the national news, the sports news, we were news junkies. We always wanted to know what is going on and what is happening.

One day, as we were sitting in the living room watching the news on television, Robert tells me, "Turn it off." He says, "It is depressing," and he only wants to think good thoughts. Absolutely! Since I am a good wife and I want him to focus on positive thoughts, I turn it off, and it is staying off for the foreseeable future. At this point in our life with all we are going through, we need to think positive and happy thoughts.

His body is beginning to show signs of the weight loss, so we keep joking with him and telling him that we are going to go on a long vacation and fatten him up with all his favorite foods. It makes him laugh, and we talk about where we have traveled and places we have gone to eat and what he would order.

Now that the decision has been made to leave his life, our family, and our marriage in God's hands, we need God to show Himself in this situation. Robert is in need of a healing, a miracle. As a family and as a couple, we are continuing to pray and believe every day.

Robert's best friend still comes and visits us every other day. I mention this not only because he is his best friend, but because he does not live close; it is a good forty-minute ride each way and that is after a full day's work. He has been such a blessing for whenever he comes, we all gather around because we need to hear the words he brings of hope and encouragement. When Robert was first diagnosed, his friend had a dream, which was rare for him. The dream was a spiral swirling around, and as it continued to spiral, a flash of light appeared, then the spiral began to swirl in the other direction.

With dreams, we never really know the meaning behind them, but for us, we held his dream close to our hearts. We always thought that the spiral was the disease and that the Lord was going to heal him and then his life would take on a different direction after the healing. Sometimes, we believe what we want to believe because it makes us feel better. But God has a plan and no matter what we think is going to change that.

Our senior pastor came to our home the night we first heard about Robert's illness. Pastor came and prayed with us as a family and told us that we would walk this road together. He is a close friend and has been a source of encouragement and visits often.

The assistant pastor comes over quite often as well. He talks with him as a pastor needs to and also serves him communion. The assistant pastor and his wife are more than our pastors, we actually counseled them before they got married as we were pre-marriage counselors. Through the years, we have become close friends, and they look at both of us as their spiritual parents. So to have him come as our spiritual child and pastor, we are very blessed.

Robert's parents stop by every few days to sit and talk with him. Usually, whenever they come, I try to go to the market as I am only leaving him for about one hour a week. I have vowed to care for him from home, as at this point, I am his nurse, caretaker, encourager, prayer partner, worship leader, best friend, and wife 24/7. When I am about to leave for the market, he gives me a list of things he is craving and wants to eat. I rush and buy them and come home and prepare them, but by that time, he doesn't want them anymore, his craving has changed to something else. This is beginning to happen more frequently as time passes.

The news of his illness is spreading to our friends, and as they hear that he is sick, they begin to visit him, and some have flown in from around the country to spend a little time with him. We have missionary friends from around the world that have called to say that they and their church are praying for a miracle. Robert is always polite and happy to see everyone when they come, but the visits are making him tired. He doesn't say much these days, as he is reserving his energy to try to breathe and get better.

His symptoms have rapidly increased, and the cancer is spreading.

Our church, North Providence Assembly of God, was holding prayer meetings every Tuesday for people to come together to pray for him and for others that are sick. My kids went regularly and said they were blessed by the number of people that were coming to pray for their dad. We are all believing for a miracle and a wonderful testimony to come from this. He wants to shout out for the Lord all that He has done for him.

I have to mention Robert's boss who has been such a blessing to our family as he has continued to send a paycheck every week to Robert and is continuing to pay for our medical insurance. Robert's friend and colleague calls me every day for updates on his condition and then passes the news around for me. He has been such a good person to lean on for me as I am able to tell him what I am feeling and going through. Another man he works with stops by regularly to chat with Robert and brings news from the jobs. He enjoys hearing about all the men and the progress of the jobs. Robert loved his job and the people he worked with, so I allow them to come even though it makes him tired.

As people visit our home, we have taken the opportunity to pray for them. We have prayed for healings in their bodies to take place, for their families, and for salvation. We have decided to use this opportunity to share the gospel and bless them as they come and visit. God has said to be ready in season and out. This may not be a good season for our family, but we use every opportunity to minister for the Lord.

As time passed, Robert began to spend time alone and became depressed. He is sleeping upright in a chair upstairs in our bedroom because he couldn't lay down due to the pain in his lungs. The longer he sat in the chair, the more uncomfortable it became; we kept adding layers of blankets to soften the seat and back for him. Actually, he was spending all his time in that chair in our bedroom. Whoever visited had to go upstairs and hang out in our bedroom. We have never had so many people in our bedroom before.

One night, as I was sleeping, I heard him talking and looked up to see him on the phone, I jumped up as it was 2:00 a.m., took the phone away from him to see who he was talking to. He was talking to his friend at work and telling him that he was going to be late to work that day. Thank God, it was his friend. I apologized, but he totally understood and was gracious about it. It was so sad and heart-wrenching to see him go through this. The doctor has increased his medication, and he was not even aware of what he was doing.

My daughter, Moriah, married to our son-in-law, Michael, has been able to be here with me every day as her company has allowed her to work from home. She has been such a blessing and support to me as she sees all that I am going through and able to help with her dad. Robert has become very quiet during the day and doesn't say more than a few words at a time as it is difficult for him to speak.

My sons, Corey and Alexander, still live at home and are able to help at nighttime with whatever has to be done. Corey spends time with his dad every night after work. They sit down and talk as men. Robert has begun to tell Corey, as the oldest male, what he wants him to do as far as the house is concerned if he doesn't make it. Alexander, as the joker in the family, has always tried to make his father laugh, but none of us are laughing much these days. Whenever we would take a family photo, Robert would hate to smile and would make this weird grin, but Alexander was the one, the only one that made him laugh hysterically.

Chapter 4

This particular weekend, Robert's family came to visit; his parents, his two brothers and their wives, as well as some friends had stopped by. They were all in our bedroom visiting as Robert would not move from his chair that we had put there for him. He was able to but was very depressed, and he chose not to move.

People would just stop in because they knew he would probably say "No" if they asked permission. That particular afternoon, we had quite a few people plus Robert, myself, and my kids in our bedroom. It was extremely overwhelming and awkward having that many people in one room. He was exhausted after the visit and became very tired.

As believers in Christ, we understand the spiritual realm, both angels and demons are present in this world. Throughout our years in ministry and being believers of Christ for as long as we have been, we have seen things happen that cannot be explained in any other way. We have seen people delivered from demon possession right in front of us while being prayed for. We have heard of angels appearing as they minister to the hurting. The spiritual realm is very real.

Okay, off my soapbox and back to my story.

In the middle of the night that followed, I was awoken by a presence in my bedroom, and I knew instantly what it was as this wasn't the first time I have seen a demon in our bedroom. I saw a demon, pacing back-and-forth at the end of my bed then leapt onto Robert as it was trying to kill him. Robert instantly sat forward trying to breath as he was being choked.

I jumped out of bed and yelled to the demon to "get out in the name of Jesus." It left instantly.

I ran to get Corey, and together, we prayed in our bedroom over Robert. Robert was breathing again and knew what had happened and said, "There was a demon in the room, and it jumped on me and began to choke me."

He said, "Go downstairs and pray down there too." We did of course. As Corey and I walked down the stairs, it was as cold as ice on the first floor, which is not normal since we have a fireplace that heats our home, and the temperature is usually around seventy-five degrees. We knew at that moment that the demon had walked through our house freely. We anointed every door and window with anointing oil and prayed over the entire house. We knew who had left the demon here in our home, and Robert told me not to let them visit again because he could not handle another episode like that.

The next morning, as Corey and I went downstairs, the air wasn't like ice any longer but had a fresh smell and feeling to it. The air smelled like a fresh sweet spring morning. We knew that the Lord had cleansed our house completely. Thank you, Jesus.

On Sunday night, the pastors and church board came over to pray for him, and as they were praying, the pastor's wife spoke a word that the Lord had given her. She said, "The Lord told her that His angels have encamped around this house because we belong to Him. This family is His, and He has put His angels here to watch over us." They knew nothing of what had just happened the night before, but God did. God surrounded our home with His angels to protect us from the demon spirits that was trying to bring harm to us.

A woman from our church, who has the gift of visions from the Lord, came over for a visit the following week. As she began to pray for Robert, she said that the Lord had shown her a vision of angels linked arm in arm completely surrounding our house. She definitely didn't know of anything that had transpired or the word spoken by the pastor's wife. God was making sure that we knew He was watching, and He was protecting us.

We have treasured all these prayers and words from God in our hearts. They bring comfort and were increasing our faith in believing for a miracle.

Weeks have passed since that whole episode with the demon, and praise the Lord, everything has been peaceful.

During the day, I have to be quiet because noise bothers Robert, so I would read my Bible for several hours every day. One day, I was reading Mark 4:35–41 where Jesus and His disciples were in the boat and a storm arose and they were frightened but Jesus was calm and actually asleep. They awoke Jesus from His nap and told Him about the storm and He said, "Silence! Be still!" Jesus calmed the storm and showed His disciples that He even controls the wind and the waves. As I read this passage, I felt that the Lord was telling me that we were in a storm of our own and all Jesus had to do was tell it to stop. I had faith that He would calm the storm surrounding us. Mark 5:1 began by them arriving on the other side of the lake, and I felt on that day that Jesus was telling me that our storm was almost over.

Due to my knee-replacement surgery only a few months ago, my knees are really hurting, having to walk up and down the stairs all day. The last couple of weeks have been exhausting for me.

"Boys, go to Grandma's house and get me a twin bed, we are moving Daddy downstairs into the living room." I said. Being his caregiver, I have to sleep right next to him in case he needs me during the night. Robert finally agreed to move downstairs and leave our bedroom. I told him it would give him more interaction with the kids and hopefully pull him out from his depression. I am now sleeping in a twin bed in the living room next to the chair he sits and sleeps in.

Robert also could not shower himself as he could not breathe due to the steam of the hot water. So as he held the oxygen mask on his face, I would have to wash him, that was until he went downstairs. After making the transition to the living room, I had begun to give him sponge baths because he did not have the strength to walk back up the stairs.

Watching my strong husband, the man I have spent my life with, go through this illness is breaking my heart. Something inside of me is growing strong as I am determined to make him well, to be the best caregiver I can be. I haven't broken down and cried since the beginning probably because I am too tired, but I also believe it is because my faith is so strong that I refuse to give in or give up.

On one afternoon, we were talking what would happen if he didn't make it. I began to have tears and jumped from my seat and put my head in his lap. He stroked my hair and my back and told me that he was surprised that I hadn't broken down sooner but that he was proud of me. He began to tell me that because I was so strong, it gave him faith and strength to push on to try to get better.

Until.

Until the cancer began to spread more, and the symptoms got worse, and now, he required oxygen 24/7. I am afraid that he was giving up. I knew that he felt horrible, and the disease had taken his strength from him as he can no longer even walk. Without mentioning all the details, I am sure you can imagine what all this means to a man, a provider, a husband, a father. Humbled to say the least.

The twin bed that we borrowed from my parents for me was in the living room, but I didn't get to sleep on it very much. Robert needed me every hour or so for pain medication, to go to the bathroom, or for whatever he needed. He would get lonely and wanted to look at me to know that he wasn't alone. Without much sleep, I had become worn out, but I loved being with my husband every minute. One morning, I went upstairs to brush my teeth and get dressed, it took me about ten minutes, and he said, "What took you so long. I missed you." Awww, it was so sweet but sad.

My heart was being torn even smaller as I watched my husband of thirty-four years being brought to this low point in his life. I know that God can heal him in a minute if that is His plan.

Hospice nurses come to the house three times a week to check on Robert's symptoms and medicine intake. This particular day, they tell both of us, "There isn't much time left, if you want to say something to each other, you need to do it soon." For the first time since his diagnosis, five months prior, I completely broke down and cried. I could not face the fact that he was dying. I refused to give up hope. I prayed as hard as I could and believed God was going to heal him.

Robert asked me to come and sit next to him as he told me, "We have loved and have been loved, I love you, Babe."

I said, "Honey, I love you too." as I found it hard to even get the words out without crying like a baby. It was hard for him to speak because the cancer had spread throughout his body now, and he couldn't breathe without the oxygen, I know all of what he meant. He had summed up our thirty-seven years together in a few words.

Less than two weeks later, on a Friday afternoon, as Moriah and I are sitting in the living room, Robert began to tell us that he was seeing faces float on the floor. I am like—oh no, not again! I jumped up and asked him what he means, and he said, "I see faces floating on the floor."

I asked him, "Are you afraid, and do I need to rebuke them?"

He said, "No, no, they are friendly faces."

We both thought that it was weird but said, "Whatever, he must be hallucinating again."

Saturday night in the middle of the night, Robert leaned over to me and said let's pray together, so of course we did. The Lord's presence was there with us as we prayed for a couple of hours together during the night. I never left his side that night.

Sunday morning, as I sat on the edge of my bed, I was so tired and could barely move. I prayed really quick and said "God, I am so tired, can you help me feel refreshed." I felt the Lord come and sit on my bed next to me and hold me in His arms, and I fell asleep for five minutes but awoke as if I had slept for eight hours. I felt so refreshed and strengthened for the day. Thank you, Lord.

As I awoke, I was looking down onto the hardwood floor in front of the twin bed where I was sleeping and saw a shadow of an angel's wing brush along the floor in front of me, instantly I turned my head to look outside thinking of the angels surrounding our home, but it was a cloudy day, so I knew it wasn't a shadow of an angel's wing. When I looked at the floor again, it happened one more time, I saw a shadow of an angel's wing brush along the floor in front of me. I asked the Lord, "What was that?" He told me that He came and held me in bed and that He was there with me.

I instantly thought in my heart of Psalm 91 and knew that the Lord wanted me to read it. I didn't recall what it said but when I went to my Bible to look it up, and it said that He holds me in His pinions, His wings, I knew that God had sat on my bed that morning with me and held me close to Himself.

With tears, I remember this moment. That God was so concerned for me that He came and held me.

> He who dwells in the shelter of the Most High
> will abide in the shadow of the Almighty.
> I will say to the Lord, "My refuge and my
> fortress, My God, in whom I trust!"
> He will cover you with His pinions (feathers), and under His wings you may seek refuge,
> His faithfulness is a shield and a solid wall of protection. (Psalm 91:1–3, 4)

Sunday night came, and I went to bed completely exhausted as Robert was really having a hard time breathing, and I had to call the doctor again to ask what I could do for him. In the middle of the night, he woke me up again, "I want to worship," he said.

"Okay, do you want to sing any song in particular?" I asked him.

He said, "Yes, I want to sing 'Holy Is the Lord.'"

I began to sing the only song I could think of.

> Holy, holy, holy! Lord God Almighty
> Early in the morning our song shall rise to Thee;
> Holy, holy holy, merciful and mighty!
> God in three Persons, blessed Trinity!

He stopped me. You are singing the wrong song, it doesn't go like that. I said then how does it go. He sang,

"Holy, holy is the Lord God. Holy, holy is the Lord God," over and over again. He sang it, but his voice was gurgling.

I said okay, I'll sing your version. We were up for a couple hours and we sang, "Holy, holy is the Lord God," until he finally fell asleep.

As I went back to bed that night I said, "Lord, if you are not going to heal him, then take him because he is suffering so much, and I can't bear to watch him in so much pain."

Monday morning came, and Corey had just left for work but wanted to stay because he knew Robert was not doing really well. But I said, "Go to work, I am here."

Chapter 5

A half hour after Corey left for work, Robert turned around and looked at me, and I jumped up and came over to him, and we just stared into each other eyes with so much love that I said, "Honey, are you okay?" After staring at me for about five minutes, his eyes rolled backward into his head, and he died in my arms. I began to scream at the top of my lungs, *"You promised me, you promised me!"* Alexander who was sleeping ran downstairs and tried to revive him. It was too late, he had already gone home. Corey raced home from work, Michael and Moriah instantly came over, and we were all there within a few minutes after he passed. We all told him how much we loved him and was going to miss him.

I couldn't let go of his body as he laid in my arms. I leaned over and put my lips onto his, and I kissed him for the last time at that moment.

Monday, January 19, 2015, at 8:20 a.m.

Robert W. Irace went home to be with the Lord.

Chapter 6

I have just lost my husband of thirty-four years, my partner in life of thirty-seven years, my best friend, my lover, and the father of my children.

In one second, I became a widow and a single mother. I felt all alone. No one to hold me in the night as I cried, no one to be intimate with, no one to have pillow talks with, and no one to share dreams with.

All of our *"our"* dreams, all of our *"our"* plans, and *"our"* future just left with him. There was no longer an *"us."*

As Robert's body was lying in the chair he passed away in, the kids and I were telling him how much we loved him. We were all crying, and I kissed him for the last time on his lips. Paramedics and policemen came to determine the time of death and to fill out all the necessary paperwork since he passed at home. The police even called the local funeral home for me and arranged for them to come and pick up his body. It took approximately two hours for them to arrive.

I called my in-laws and then my parents. My parents had stayed home here in Rhode Island until the beginning of January but went to Florida for one week, and that happened to be the week that he passed. I called them, and they instantly jumped on the next plane and were here the following morning. My younger sister and brother-in-law who live in Washington State were also here the following day and were thoughtful enough to purchase a plaque in Robert's honor, and it hangs next to the door at our church. My older sister and brother-in-law live in Maine near the Canadian border; they drove down for the services. My brother lives next door to me and came over as soon as he heard that Robert had passed away. It was wonderful to have family close by.

In the meantime, our pastors and close friends came instantly, and thank God, they did. I could not have helped my children deal with their grief and anger as I was having a hard-enough time myself. As the funeral home personnel came to remove his body, they asked us not to watch and asked me if I wanted his face covered or not while they were leaving. I said, "No, leave his face exposed," which was a mistake. My kids were looking out the window and saw Robert's face as he was being taken out on the stretcher. It was the last time he would ever be here in our home, and the last time that he was to go through our front door.

In that very moment, I saw my pastors and friends hold my children close as they screamed, swung their fists, and exhibited all that was inside of them. My children were extremely upset and angry when he passed. Both of my boys punched something in my home and made holes in a wall and a cupboard that Robert had built for me. I was at first angry that they were destroying our home, but I understood that they didn't know how else to get it out. I still have a hole in my dining room wall that needs to be repaired, I have since covered the hole with a picture.

Our senior pastor and his wife even came to the funeral home with us to choose a coffin and plan the services. They truly did walk this journey with us as they have not left our side the entire way.

During Robert's illness, I believed God was going to heal him, I prayed and prayed, I couldn't have prayed any more or any harder. Obviously, it was not God's will. No matter how hard I prayed, believed, or how much I asked the Lord, His will always prevails. Even though I don't like His decision or agree with it, I have no choice but to accept it; I can't change it or do anything about it. Robert has no more pain, in fact, he is in the presence of the Almighty rejoicing and singing with the angels.

I realized that the scripture in Mark was for Robert. His storm has ended, and he did reach the other side safely, and He is with the Lord. For me, my storm was still swirling.

The week of the funeral—I was numb. I couldn't believe this was happening. We held the calling hours at our church, where approximately one-thousand-five-hundred people came to show their respects. Every person had a story to tell me of how my husband had touched them and their family. My children and I were overwhelmed by the support from all these people.

In preparation for the funeral, we looked through boxes of old photographs and shared wonderful memories with each other as we put together a slideshow to share with everyone who attended that day.

Walking behind the coffin that held the body of my husband, realizing that this was the last day I will be with his body until I see him in heaven was an overwhelming feeling, and my body began to shake and convulse. All of the emotions that I had held back during the week preparing for the funeral had hit me all at once, and I couldn't control it any longer.

At Robert's funeral, Moriah and Corey both wanted to honor their father and tell some stories that most people wouldn't know. Robert was a very funny man and was an excellent father, and they wanted everyone to know. Alexander stood with Robert's best friend, as he spoke and shared his memories of Robert. Our assistant pastor also shared personal remarks and memories of how Robert had touched his life and mentored him through his journey. Our senior pastor shared a message of hope and salvation as well as personal remarks. All of them poured their heart into what they said and gave Robert a great tribute. The funeral was on January 22, 2015, which also happened to be Corey's 25th birthday. Instead of celebrating like most people do at that age, he was saying goodbye to his father.

The day of the funeral, every seat of the church was occupied, and the procession to the cemetery had many cars. The funeral director told me after that this was the largest funeral that he had ever done. The procession of cars had to cross through three towns to get to the cemetery so the police escorted us as well as had police posted and stopped traffic at every intersection along the way.

Standing next to my husband's coffin at his burial site, our senior pastor said a few final words and asked everyone to think of one word that would remind them of Robert. That whenever they would hear this word, they would instantly think of him. I only had to think for a moment for I knew what my word was. My word was "*beloved*." He was my beloved husband, he was my world, my everything. In our bedroom over our bed, I had cross-stitched a scripture and Robert had made and painted the frame. The scripture was, "My beloved is mine, and I am His." (Song of Solomon 2:16).

After we returned home from the luncheon, the funeral director stopped by and delivered all the flowers that were left behind. As it was January and snow was coming the next day, they could only leave a few pieces at the cemetery. We all picked some roses to dry, and the rest I threw out. I couldn't stand looking at and smelling flowers any longer. The following day, we took them all to the town transfer station. I felt bad because they were beautiful flowers, but I couldn't do it one more day, one more minute. I needed to move past the funeral and all the reminders.

Before the calling hours, I had prayed over the coffin that God would still do a miracle and raise him from the dead. I was thinking, *Wow, what a testimony that would be.* "Come on, God, this will bring You glory." I couldn't stop believing that somehow, God was going to do a miracle. I lived a fairy-tale life, and there is no way that it could end this way. "Come on, God," I kept praying and hoping.

I sat on the arm of my couch and would look down the driveway as I was expecting him to walk up the driveway at any minute. At times, I would open the door and hope he was standing there. I did this for about a month. After the month, it hit me. I had been in denial, and he was not coming back. He was gone. I am all alone.

Watching Robert whittle down from a strong healthy man to a thin, sick man was devastating, but strength rose up inside of me to take care of him and do whatever I had to make him well and comfortable. But now, there was no one to be strong for; I felt weak, defeated, lost, abandoned, forgotten, lonely, and so many more descriptions, but you get the point.

All I kept thinking and even told a friend. I don't know how to be a widow, there isn't a widow guidebook. I don't even know if what I'm going through is normal. What is coming next in my grief? How long does it last? What do I do with the anger? How long does the loneliness last, will I ever get used to it? What do I do to get my life back to "normal?"

The night of the funeral, my family purchased food for all of us to eat. Everyone was here in my home and sitting at the dining room table. We prayed, and everyone started to eat except I felt sick to my stomach. I couldn't eat a bite. I started to bawl my eyes out, and my body was shaking. I was sitting in Robert's seat at the head of the table and realized all at once that he would never sit there again.

When you lose someone that means so much, there is a huge void in your life, and you have to experience and go through so many little things that other people have no idea. Being a widow is not easy, and unless they have gone through it, they do not understand, they are sad, but they do not understand. I was the first widow in our family, not the first in our church but the first one for a few years, and no one knows what to do with me and for me, so they did nothing.

When I read my Bible, all I could read was Psalms, it was soothing and comforting like a blanket wrapped around me. I would lay in bed and read, I would wake up and read. I needed the pain to stop. I know God had the answers in the Word. God became my husband, not in a physical way, but in a way that may be hard for some to understand. I would lay in bed at night and talk with the Lord softly and share my heart or moan with my face in my pillow. During the day, when feelings would overwhelm me, I would scream outside or yell because I didn't know what else to do, words wouldn't come at times.

A couple months after Robert had passed away, I went and had lunch with a friend. She mentioned to me about a story she had heard on a Christian TV show about a little boy dying and what he saw. I was interested in reading his story because I began to wonder; what was Robert doing in heaven, was he really there, and things like that. I went to our local bookstore, and with this book on my mind, I went to find it, and when I found it, I opened up the book in the middle just to read a passage. What I read was astounding. All I read was that the boy when he arrived in heaven heard the angels singing, "Holy, holy is the Lord God. Holy, holy is the Lord God."

I realized at that moment that the day before Robert died, he had begun to hear the angels singing, and God had confirmed to me that he was with Him, and he was okay. As I read these lines, I caught myself because I almost fell over onto the floor in the bookstore. The emotions that had been racing through me for the past month or so all came to a head at that very moment.

After realizing and assured that Robert was in heaven, I began to wonder, what was he doing up there? Was he talking to Moses, hanging out with Samson, who knows but my thoughts of him being in heaven began to settle down with my heart and mind. Knowing that he was okay and that the Lord took the time to let me know that by showing me that particular passage in the book that was recommended to me by a friend.

Chapter 7

For the past two summers, we have had small black moths in our bedroom, no other room in the house would have them and not during the day, but every night, we had these small black moths. It would vary as to how many we had; some nights, it was only a few, and other nights, there were a couple dozen. Robert would get a towel and hit them off the ceiling, then I would have to clean them up. The summer after he passed, the moths started again, and I would get a towel and swing at them. I am only 5'3" so I had trouble reaching the ceiling with a towel, but I would still swing at them. I swear they were laughing at me. I would get a footstool that I have in my room, step on it, swing the towel, step down, move the footstool, swing the towel, again and again until all the moths were gone. Night after night, the moths came back.

My shoulder began to bother me from swinging the towel every night a couple dozen times. One night, I had had it, I said, "Lord, if Robert was here, he would be killing the moths for me. He is with You now, so You are my husband now, I need You to get rid of these moths for me once and for all." Don't you know, after that night—I have not had one moth in my bedroom. God went to the source and took care of it for me.

As I look back, it makes me wonder if we had to endure the moths so God could show me that He was taking care of me. Because no other room ever had them in the whole house, just my bedroom. It is strange to think about, but God is the God of the miraculous. He loves to show us His wonder working power and how much He loves us. Even by getting rid of the moths and saving my shoulder from pain, from the frustration of having to do it every night during the summer. God is amazing, and He cares for each of us. Especially those who are hurting. God began to show me that He would be taking care of me, that He was my husband while mine was gone.

I had no desire to eat let alone cook or even go to the grocery store. The last thing I wanted to do was run into somebody that I knew. I didn't want to have to explain what happened or how I was feeling. I just wanted to get in and get out unnoticed.

My two boys are still living at home with me, and I needed to feed them, but I couldn't even feed myself. I stopped cooking, I stopped caring about life, I didn't care about my responsibilities, all I wanted was the pain to go away. Both of my boys like to eat, they were twenty-five and nineteen, they began to buy pizza and take-out food and eating very unhealthily. I would eat cereal or scrambled eggs every day, I didn't care, I can't say that enough.

When Robert was sick, we had visitors all the time. People were always coming and going, they would bring food, desserts, things that the boys would eat. After Robert had passed, people brought over food—lots of food, we received fruit baskets. Now that the funeral is over, no one comes over, no one calls, we are left to fend for ourselves. I know that everyone has their own life to live, and life does move on, well not for me. I was not able to move on. I was in a full-blown depression.

I would go to the market and feel overwhelmed the minute I walked through the door. I would walk down two aisles and then straight to the checkout. Upon coming home, I would carry in two bags of groceries, and the boys would say, "Mom, is that all you bought?"

"Yup, I couldn't handle any more aisles." I would apologize over and over.

Macaroni and cheese for supper again.

Pizza again.

Cereal again.

Scrambled eggs again.

"Mom, we need to eat," they had begun to say. "Mom, you need to eat."

Food became unappealing to me, and I just didn't care to even look at it. I felt bad for the boys but couldn't do anything about it. This continued for about three months.

As the warm weather approached, I needed some shorts and summer clothes. As the summer before, I had the double knee-replacement surgery and couldn't leave the house and especially when Robert became sick. So it had been two summers since I had purchased any summer clothing, and I really needed some. Mine were worn out and looking like rags.

One day, I felt brave, so I set out to go to a local clothing store to purchase just a couple pairs of shorts. I actually drove to the plaza not far from my house but couldn't walk into the store. I began to panic and drove to a different parking lot and just sat there and cried. Then went home. No shorts. The next day, I tried it again, I actually went into the store's parking lot and sat there. But then, went home.

What is the matter with me, I am an interior designer, and I shop in these stores all the time for my job, I began to think. By the third day, I made it inside the store and found a couple pairs of shorts and a couple tops, but the one thing I feared happened, I ran into someone I knew. She was gracious, and we spoke for only a couple minutes because she sensed that I was struggling. I checked out and came right home. Back to my safety net. Back to my cocoon that I have known now for almost a year. I was home for a year as my rehabilitation was for one month after my surgery followed by the six months that Robert was sick and five months after he had passed. I have not been out of the house for more than minutes at a time in just under twelve months. I am feeling overwhelmed at these new challenges that I am facing alone.

During the winter months, I sat in my chair in front of the television and watched sitcoms that I have never watched before just to make myself laugh and get my mind off of my life. I watched series of shows so that I could wonder about the life of the character on TV rather than my own. It was like I was living through them. I wondered how each situation they found themselves in would turn out.

I had put together every jigsaw puzzle that I owned at least three times, and my kids were tired of seeing me sit in front of a puzzle. It was an activity that was occupying my mind, my thoughts, and was helping me cope with time. One thing about time is that it keeps moving whether you want it to or not. No one can stop time, or make it speed up, or slow it down; it is what it is.

Even though I had spent so much time at home, I avoided my bedroom. At night, I would go to bed between 2:00 to 3:00 a.m. I would wait until I couldn't stay awake any longer then go to bed and sleep for only a few hours and would be up again early in the morning before the kids left for their day. Unable to face the loneliness and the absence of intimacy without my husband lying there by my side, no pillow talk, no private moments, no brushing of bodies in the kitchen when no one else was looking, no one to kiss or hug me. That part of my life was gone, had died and was buried with Robert. He was the only man that I had ever been intimate with. He was my first boyfriend, my first love, my husband, best friend, lover, confidant, my partner in life, the one who shared my dreams, my encourager, the father of my children, the one who made me laugh and could calm me with a hug.

One particular night, I couldn't bear the pain and the loneliness any longer. At 2:00 a.m., with both boys sound asleep in their rooms, I walked into the kitchen and took a knife from the drawer and laid it on the counter. Instantly, I felt God say to me, "Is this really what you want for your children, to lose you too?" I put the knife away and went to bed. The next morning. I told all three of my children what had happened, and they knew that I had reached my deepest darkest moment so far. Months later, they told me that they thought they "were going to bury me not long after Daddy had passed."

That night, my life changed.

I knew that God was there with me.

I knew that He spoke to me.

That all along, He had been watching me but allowing me to work through my emotions and feelings. God came to my deepest, darkest moment and carried me out. He met me where I was. He put me in His arms and carried me. My love for the Lord has grown because of that moment in time—that moment in my life. I now know that the Lord has walked this journey with me. I believe that I had to get to that point to know that God is walking with me, is watching over me, is taking care of me and is concerned for me. That He still has a plan for me, and I had to go that low in order to grow.

Luke 7:47 says, "The woman who had great sin was forgiven, she loved great, but the one who has been forgiven of little sin loves little."

This scripture always bothered me because I felt that I was a good girl growing up, lived a good life that I didn't have much to be forgiven of, but I truly loved the Lord. After this night, I knew that the Lord had forgiven me for my thoughts that night, and they were not good thoughts. He came and stopped me, He came and forgave me, He came and loved me, and now, I love Him with a deeper love than I have ever known. That scripture came alive and true to me that night. I had more sin than I thought, pride—to think that my life was my own, it wasn't as I had given it to the Lord thirty years earlier.

I didn't think I mattered much to God because I was left alone for months with no answer to any of my prayers. The nights I would lie in bed and just scream into my pillow and weep with tears that would physically hurt because they were so big and so many. The days that I would walk outside in the backyard and scream like a baby because I had no more words to say, the pain was unbearable, and I was mad at my situation. I couldn't believe that this was my life. You never think that it will happen to you, at least I never did.

I always thought I was living a fairy tale. I had the perfect life, a wonderful husband, three great kids, a son-in-law, parents, and a family that was very supportive of all that we did. Robert and I used to have people come over to us whether in church or out socializing that they had watched us and could tell how much in love we were with each other, and they wish they had that kind of relationship.

We ministered at our church where we had attended for over thirty years. He was the youth pastor, and I was his wife. We began the youth ministry at our church and was faithful to that ministry for twelve years. Both of us had a part to play in the ministry just like everything else we did, we did it together. Robert would prepare and deliver the messages twice a week. I would plan, advertise, and arrange all the details of our weekly activity events. Each of us put in approximately twenty hours a week into our portion of the ministry.

I had become shy and hidden behind my husband and found it difficult to speak publicly. I knew that it wasn't my gift to speak publicly, that is why Robert chose to do all of the messages. I wasn't like that at home, but for some reason, I became shy in public. I think it was because he was always the life of the party. Whenever we would walk into a room, he was the person everyone flocked to and wanted to be next to. He had all the jokes and one-liners that made everyone laugh. I became invisible.

After twelve years and feeling it was time, we stepped down from youth ministry. The ministry had grown from the four teenagers we began with to fifty-six teenagers coming out three times a week. At that time, the ministry needed a full-time youth pastor, which we did not feel that was our calling. After a few years passed, we began to help couples that were engaged and prepare them for marriage. As we had been happily married for thirty-four years, we had the tools to help other couples begin their journey on solid ground. We began doing small groups of couples for about two years, but as the need arose, we started to do individual couple counseling. With many of these couples, one of them were part of our youth ministry so we knew them well, and it was an honor to usher them into this next portion of their life. We were very involved in our church and loved it.

We had always done ministry together as a couple. Now, I was facing serving the Lord alone for the first time. I didn't think that God could use me as I found it hard to speak to people and could never begin or carry a conversation. The words never came to what to say. But life has changed for me where Robert is no longer here, I had to face the Lord and stand alone.

"God, what is your plan for me?" I began to ask Him.

My heart had broken into such small pieces, ashes actually, when something dies it turns into ashes. My heart had died. God had taken all my ashes—my little pieces, the crumbs that were left—and began reconstructive surgery on my heart and life.

After six months or so, I began to devour the Word, dig into the meanings behind it, the history of each story; I began to have questions I never had before. I never had the question of "why" but questions about the Word. Those questions led me to dig deeper and deeper. As I read more and more—God wasn't healing my heart— He was creating a new one inside of me. One that began to love Him deeper and more intimate. I began a deeper, more intimate relationship with my Father, Jesus, and the Holy Spirit.

Chapter 8

When you lose someone close to you, there is the instant grieving, but what most people don't see or understand is you have to go through the year of firsts.

That first year without the one you love is very difficult. You have to face all the memories you had made during each holiday, each season of the year without them. Here in New England, the seasons are very pronounced. Winter is a time of relaxing your body while gearing up for the spring, summer, and fall.

In the winter, we used to spend time shoveling after each snow storm, carrying in wood for our fireplace that we had spent most of the spring and summer cutting, and enjoying family time as we were all indoors together. We would watch football, hockey, then March Madness, golf, and any other sport that was on television. We would make jigsaw puzzles, play board games, and have times of just sitting around and conversing and laughing together as a family.

Valentine's Day is a special day for romance and couples expressing the feelings for one another. It was hard watching as other couples celebrate their love, which they should be doing, but all I had was a trip to the cemetery with a single red rose that I left for him.

Spring was a time of opening up the windows, shutting down the fireplace, and cleaning the house because the fireplace burns wood all winter, and the dust from the ashes needs to be cleaned. I would do the weekly cleaning, but in the spring, the walls would get washed, the curtains would get washed and rehung, the windows would get cleaned, and everything would feel and smell clean. Once the house was finished, outside we would go. It was time to refresh the flower beds with new annuals and a fresh layer of cocoa shell mulch. We would set up the porch furniture every year, but it would be too cold to enjoy it.

Summer was a wonderful time at our house; we would spend all of our time on the porch. We would cook on the grill and eat our meals outside. Platters of fresh fruit, cheese and crackers, grilled pizza, along with burgers and hotdogs, shish kebabs and any other grilled delight would be enjoyed. We would lay on the porch, turn on the music and absorb the sunshine, then take a dip in the pool, then back into the sunshine, then back into the pool. You get the idea; this would go on all day, especially on Sunday after church. Our yard required a good amount of daily maintenance, but we enjoyed doing it together.

When our church began Saturday night services, we would attend especially during the summertime so we could enjoy one full day as a family together. Sunday mornings, we would make a pot of coffee, bring the porch chairs under the big oak tree in our backyard, and sit there talking about our future plans. As the kids woke up, one by one, they would come out and sit under the tree with us. We had spent many Sundays as a family sitting in a circle under this tree, laughing and talking about the events of the week and plans for the next. Robert and I would talk about our upcoming vacation plans, retirement dreams of traveling, what needed to be done around the house that particular year, what the yard looked like and how we could make it better. We were always working in our yard to make it look better and better. It seemed as if it was always a work in progress, always a job or a new part of the yard getting a face-lift. We would talk about future plans to have a house in another state where it was warmer during the winter. Robert always wanted to move, and I always wanted to be near the kids. It was a constant discussion that would always end with, we will just have to see what happens when we retire.

We would make plans for that particular summer, we would choose a project or two. Brick walkways, landscape, shrubs, trees, flowers, stone walls, fences, garden and toolshed, woodshed, power washing the porch, painting the house, whatever it was, we were always talking about it, and every year, we would begin another project or two.

We have many memories about each project, what made us want to do it, what was the reason we had to do it in the first place, and all the complications, decisions, and elbow grease it took to accomplish it. The ironic part of all of this is that we live 750' off the main road, and no one can even see our house and yard unless they drive up our very long and secluded driveway. We did all of this work because we enjoyed the process, we enjoyed being outside, working together, and mainly because it is what made us happy.

Robert would gather materials from the jobs that he was on. At the end of each job, they would be throwing away things, and he would just ask if he could have them, and we accumulated a ton of stuff! One year, he was working on a high school in our state, and at the end of the job, they had bricks left over, so he asked the bricklayer if he could have the leftover bricks. The man not only said that he could have them but delivered them to our house. Our brick walkway leading to our front door are the bricks from that local high school. The bricks from our back walkway leading to our porch were from another job that he was on and had in a pile in the woods for a few years until we decided what to do with them.

At one time, we had a vegetable garden. I love to garden and plant flowers, herbs, and vegetables. So we decided one year that we were going to make it one of our projects. As a designer, I couldn't just clean out the land and plant, we needed to have a beautiful garden. Robert built seven large raised beds for me to plant vegetables and herbs in. These boxes were four feet wide, eight feet long, and twelve inches deep. We designed them into a pattern, one in the back and then two up the sides and two at angles in the front to make a circle with two in the center. We filled the beds with loom we purchased from a farm, so it was rich in nutrients. We bought red stones to lay between the beds so the weeds wouldn't come up.

Then, we decided to put a white vinyl picket fence with special posts and caps at each section. We encountered a problem because we only put the fence up on two sides because it was very pricey, and the other two sides were woods. We felt that it looked nice and separated the vegetable garden from the rest of the yard with the fence, it served its purpose. The following year, we built the garden and toolshed for our lawn mower and garden tools. We even laid a beautiful brick walkway to go from the yard through the gate on the fence down to the garden. Robert created two more flower beds for me at the entrance of the garden and put a short stonewall on one side as a retainer for the dirt.

All excited, I went and bought flats of vegetables and packets of seeds to plant. I filled in all the raised boxes with these plants and seeds. I would go out every day to water them, weed them, tie up the tomatoes as they began to grow. But then, it happened. The animals thought that we had planted the garden for them, the deer would come out every night and eat away. The chipmunks and squirrels would nibble at whatever they wanted. One year, we had bunny rabbits, cute, but they like to eat everything. No worries, they only lasted one year as a fox took care of that problem for us. No more rabbits the next year.

Robert was very inventive and would think of ways to get the deer to stop coming in our yard. We hung ivory soap from trees, we drilled holes in bars and bars of ivory soap and strung it with twine and tied it to the branches around our yard and especially in the vegetable garden. No, that didn't work, they liked our vegetables too much. They must have thought I had planted them just for them to fill their bellies. I always wondered what a conversation would be between the animals, "Hey, that lady in the back, she planted a garden for us to eat from, help yourself." Laughable but frustrating.

One year, he thought he figured out the best idea yet. We bought aluminum pie plates, lots of them, and poked a hole in each of them and strung them with twine and placed them along the garden where we thought they were coming in. You have to picture this because it was hysterical. He wired a motion detector up in the big tree that we sat underneath on Sunday mornings. The motion detector triggered a hose to turn on a sprinkler to shoot water onto the pie plates, and the noise would scare the deer away.

Every night, we had to hook up the hose, turn the water on, make sure the sprinkler was in the right direction, every night; did I say every night? It became another chore, and it did work for a while until the deer caught on. Once they realized that it was the noise from the pie plates and that they weren't going to get squirted, they began to eat again. In the meantime, we spent the entire summer with pie plates strung up along our fence and a water hose and sprinkler set up across the lawn every night. He was a master at creating something he needed out of what he had. He would have been okay living in the early days, I used to tell him.

Then one day, I noticed Alexander, who always had a bat or a golf club in his hand and was responsible for many broken things in our house. He broke the glass on my lantern that is next to my garage door a few times, I have lost count. He used to practice his batting against my garage door, he said, "I'm only using tennis balls." If you could see my garage door, you would question it too. My door looked like the face of a golf ball with all the craters. Well, back to what I was saying; one day, I was sitting on my back porch and saw something on my fence and walked over to see what it was, and I couldn't believe what I saw. Alexander had been practicing his golf swing in the backyard and he missed the woods a couple of times because he put holes in my white vinyl fence that was surrounding my vegetable garden.

When I confronted him, he told me that Dad knew, and Dad said, "Don't tell your mother."

Well, obviously, Alexander didn't stop there because the following year, I found two craters in the side of our above ground pool. You can imagine how upset I got that day. He told me that Dad knew about those too. I just shook my head and laughed. What else was I supposed to do with that?

Well, I hate to say it, but after about five years, we gave up on the vegetable garden idea, sold the white vinyl fence online to a local family, and pulled up all the boxes and planted grass. We never removed the bricks that led into the garden, and to this day, they are still there as a reminder of what once was there. We call it the walkway to nowhere. It is really cool looking to see a brick walkway going through two flower beds with stonewalls, and it leads now to more grass.

Robert had started a stonewall down the driveway; well, I should say that he piled stones up along the driveway whenever we would dig one up. Some projects were left unfinished.

As you can imagine, after being together for thirty-seven years, we have many memories. It is wonderful to think back over the memories that we have made together, both good and bad, funny and sad. The part that I am struggling with is not having him here to reminisce with, as well as not being able to make any more with him. As a widow, the loneliness is front and center all the time. I find myself thinking over a memory and want to laugh with him or say to him, "Do you remember when?" but then, I look to the chair where he would always sit, and it is empty. Emotions begin to well up inside of me all over again. I want to laugh from the memory and cry because I miss him.

That first summer, the kids and I tackled our first big project together. We took some cabinets that Robert had gathered and was planning on installing a work area in our garage since we only have a crawl space for a basement. Robert loved woodworking and creating things like furniture and cabinets for me. It was his dream to have a workshop with an actual workbench in it. All we ever had was a folding table. So we managed to lay out half of the garage into a work area with a workbench. My father, my brother, father-in-law, and brother-in-law helped in the construction and electrical parts. The kids and I put up the sheetrock, and we taped and mudded. It was not perfect, but we made it work. Then, I painted the walls a pretty yellow, so it would bring joy whenever we walked into the garage. I had a green sign made with yellow lettering that said, "DAD'S WORKSHOP" along with a picture of a screwdriver as he was an electrician. We hung the sign over the cabinets along with his hard hat from work and a couple of antique oil cans he had collected. There was even an antique flour mill that my father-in-law made into a light for me.

The first time I went to the store to buy a card for my parents' anniversary, it hit me hard, knowing that I would never purchase another anniversary card for Robert, and I would never be able to have a golden anniversary. I began to cry in the middle of the market and had to leave because I couldn't control it. These are the little things that people don't understand unless you have gone through it. You would think, just buy the card for your parents, but it is so much more than that. To think for thirty-four years, I would go and buy Robert a card for our anniversary which we would take away on our mini vacation and give to each other. We would write inside of the card sentiments how we felt about each other. Words that I have reread and cherish deeply. Feelings from my husband's heart that he penned for my eyes only. The year he passed away would have been thirty-five years of marriage for us, a milestone, and realizing that day purchasing the card for my parents that even if I got married again, I am too old to ever have a fiftieth golden anniversary. It is a milestone that every couple looks forward to, and it is something that is unattainable to me and that made me emotional, feeling defeated, empty, and even more alone. I know that we would have made it fifty years as we were very much in love with each other and enjoyed each other's company. That is my only consolation.

Fall was always our favorite time of year. The air became crisp and was comfortable to work in. We would go apple picking, art festivals, country fairs, and antique shopping, as well as taking a small vacation to celebrate our anniversary as we were married in November. We would take day trips or sneak away for a weekend, and we would find remote places to be alone. This one time, he knew that I wanted to dance with him, so we found a gazebo in a parking lot, and we danced and didn't care as people drove by. We used to drive around and look for out-of-the-way coffee shops to sit and relax in. We truly loved just being together, and we made many special memories, and I am thankful that I have them to remember.

When I began to think about removing my wedding rings, I was torn and asked God what I should do about removing my wedding rings. I specifically prayed and asked the Lord, "Do you have someone else for me?" As I was opening the closet door to get my coat to leave for church that evening, I banged my hand on the door and my rings broke apart. I have banged my hand many times over the course of thirty-four years, but why was today different? I knew God had just answered my question. You see, ten years earlier, I was tired of my rings spinning around my finger, so I had them welded together, but God just broke them apart.

I wasn't ready to remove them that day, and I decided that I would wait until the one-year anniversary of his passing. The day after his one-year anniversary, I did; I went to the cemetery and came home and removed them. Removing my wedding rings was tough. It was realizing that the covenant made with Robert on our wedding day was done. No longer in effect. Never to be with him again as his wife. In heaven, we will be together but not as husband and wife. That was hard to swallow, and it took me time to come to terms with it. So I took my rings off. The outline of the absence of the rings is evident on my finger, a constant reminder that they are missing, that he is missing. My rings are off, the indent is still there, but I know in my heart that there will be another ring there some day, for I believe that the Lord answered my question that day.

Our fall would begin on Columbus Day weekend, when the local art festivals begin. For a couple weekends in October, we would meet as a family, Robert and I, my children, and my parents would go to a favorite breakfast place before heading to the festival held on historical property about an hour from our home. This was always a family favorite every year. The smell of kettle corn being popped was in the air wherever you went. The food court area was full of trucks selling their meals and treats. Corn dogs was always our favorite, we would get one every year and only at this particular truck at this festival. So the first year I went without Robert, I did get a corn dog, but for some reason, it didn't have the same meaning as previous years. The following year, I chose not to get one, to avoid the emotion of it and the extra calories.

At these festivals, we had made friends with some of the vendors selling their wares, and we would always stop and visit with them. The first year without Robert, I went and said hello but found myself explaining my situation over and over again. It was exhausting, but I made it through the day, and knew I wouldn't have to explain it again next year and to guarantee that I made sure I saw everyone and got it out of the way.

Owning a home in New England, fall was a busy time of year as we needed to prepare for the upcoming winter. We heat our home with firewood and had ordered some from a local distributor, which was a first for me as Robert always knew somewhere to get the wood. This year, I had to locate someone who had already cut and split the wood and had them deliver it to us. Robert was a master at making something out of nothing; he had taken corrugated metal that some-one gave us and built a covering for the firewood. The boys and I spent time stacking the wood in that little section Robert had built.

You never realize how many chores or jobs a person does until you have to do them yourself. I was used to doing my chores and errands and knew where to go and who to see, but Robert's chores I did not know. I found myself exhausted most of the time, both phys-ically and mentally. Winter is not going to wait until I am ready for it; it comes when it comes, and I need to be ready or we are going to be really cold this year. That is not an option in my mind.

The holidays were difficult as there was a definite empty spot at the table. Robert's personality would fill a room and make every-one laugh. He always sat at the head of the table, and no one has sat there since he passed, it remains empty. My children didn't want to celebrate or acknowledge the holidays, but we did as I knew we needed to.

That first Christmas morning, my kids and I sat around the tree like normal and started opening gifts like robots then stopped as one by one walked away. We did not resume to open gifts until later in the day. It was knowing we needed to push through the emo-tions and face it but on the other hand he was sorely missed. My sister-in-law had crocheted a Santa hat for Robert as he was the one who always handed out the gifts whenever the whole family was here on Christmas day. She crocheted his name "BOB" on the hat but it looked more like "808." His brothers joked about it every year and nicknamed him "808" as the Bs looked like the number 8. Every Christmas for the past ten years or so, his name was 808. His broth-ers would come over on Christmas Day and tease him by saying something like, "Hey, 808, where's your hat?" That year, his hat was placed on the back of a small chair that I have in my living room.

No one put it on or would even touch it. There was no laughing or joking that Christmas. My kids were there, and no one even wanted to open a gift. About half way through, one by one, they just got up and walked away not able to handle their emotions.

I remember going to bed that night and just crying into my pillow. I had held it in all day, trying to stay strong for my kids. Letting them know that they can make it, that I can make it, so they wouldn't worry about me. I was so glad that the day was *over*! The memories of that Christmas I would love to forget.

At Robert's funeral, many people had said that they would be there to help, but sadly, I know that was just words because no one ever came around to help. The only exception was his best friend and a man he worked with came and did some electrical work for me. Everyone has their own lives to live, I understand, but for a new widow, I was struggling to figure out some of the chores Robert always did. I didn't want to always ask my boys to do everything. I felt it was my responsibility, and I struggled through it, and little by little, God showed me what had to be done. And by the grace of God, my two boys and myself we made it through the first winter, we kept the fireplace going and the wood stacked.

At times, I felt that no one understood me. I was going through situations, feelings, and emotions that no one in my family or friends had gone through. Only God could give me the comfort that I needed. I talked, cried, screamed, leaned on, depended on for *everything*. I walked this journey with God alone. I didn't go back to church for six months. It took me a few months to get my head together to be able to make it through the day without crying all the time. When I did go back, I was strong; strong for my kids, trying to be an example. I started worshiping at the altar, mainly to hide. That sounds opposite of what it should, but if I couldn't see anyone during worship when I felt that no one could see my tears, my emotions, my hurts and pains. That I would slip into church, worship without anyone noticing, and slip out just as quietly. Well, let's say God had other plans.

I found out months later as people began to tell me that they were watching me, their hearts were broken for me, they watched from afar as they watched God begin to do a work in me. From crying during service, to being a woman who would get so into worship that others were drawn in just because they were looking at me. That they were encouraged to see that if I could worship God after what I had been through, that they could too.

I will tell you later all that God has shared with me and done in my life.

It seemed with every special occasion and the different people I met throughout the year, it was similar to checking off boxes on a list. I couldn't wait until the one-year anniversary was over, so I could breathe again.

Chapter 9

Small town America, that is where I grew up. Everyone knew your name, where you lived, and who your family was. Main street had a few small shops, a local post office, a pharmacy, and a general store that sold penny candy. My parents would give us a quarter whenever we went to the general store. We would walk out with a small paper bag with all of our goodies sticking out of the top. My brother and two sisters would eat theirs pretty quickly, but I always rationed mine out to last the whole week. There was even "the mall" which consisted of one large wooden building with a few departments inside as well as a cafe. My first job as a teenager was inside "the mall" in the department that sold wood products like bird feeders, paper towel holders, napkin dispensers, and the like. Other departments in "the mall" were clothing and shoes.

I was what you would call a tomboy. I rode my bike around the neighborhood with all the boys (there were no girls my age). We played games together every day after school, and the boys were my friends. The street where I lived was a dirt road where they would put oil down once during the summer to help the dirt become hard. The neighborhood kids all played kick ball or other games in the street because there were about five cars a day that went by. Today, if you played in the street, you would be hit by a car as we have about five cars every minute going by.

I took dance lessons from a local woman who would teach all the children and then do a recital at the end of the year. I took tap and baton lessons. As I became a teenager, I walked in parades twirling my baton and throwing it in the air, I was quite talented. I also marched in other parades; the local 4th of July parade is really big in our small town where everyone comes out with their lawn chairs and coolers and cheer as the floats or marching bands go by. One year, my girl troop covered a Volkswagen bug with aluminum foil to look like a spaceship, and the girls, including me, were painted blue and dressed as Martians.

I attended youth group at our church every Sunday night. The leaders always shared a lesson as well as allowing us activity time. When I was eleven years old, I went to a Billy Graham movie with my youth group and gave my life to the Lord that night and got water baptized a short time afterward. I have known the Lord for forty-five years but only served Him for the past thrity-three as I rededicated my life as an adult. I believe because I made an early commitment my youth was free from sex and drugs.

I played women's softball when I was thirteen to fifteen years old and ended up being the manager with my aunt as none of the other ladies wanted to do it. I was good at organizing and encouraging others from a young age. I could always see the potential in other people and was never afraid of telling them.

But not all my memories of growing up were good ones. I remember getting dressed in my new uniform and heading out to my first night of this girl troup, I was seven years old, and as I walked into the home where the meetings were held, some of the other girls were cruel and said some things to me that were not nice about my appearance. It made such an impression on me that I have never forgotten that moment. Another time was when I began middle school, because our town is so small, we joined with another town for middle and high school. Within the first couple of weeks, some of the girls from the other town obviously didn't like me because they threw tomatoes at me on the playground. To this day, I have never eaten a raw tomato.

Because of these girls and situations, I had a distaste for girls and would rather hang out with the boys. They don't judge you for what you look like. Until high school when all the boys want girls for girlfriends. That is when I had to become friendly with everyone but not really a friend to anyone. I never had a female "best friend," that special someone you could confide in or stay up late with and talk with about boys and things.

In high school, I was involved in many activities, I ran on the girls track team for two years, which I was not that good at, so I became the manager of the team, and I also played on the intramural girls field hockey team. I was the founder and editor in chief of our high school's newspaper where I had reporters and photographers working for me. I was the secretary of our annual dance show, which was a huge event in our school, as well as the president of a special program that was held at our high school.

Even though I was very involved, it filled in my time but not the void in my heart. I had always longed to have someone special and be someone special to them. Then, it happened.

In October of my senior year in high school, I met Robert; he was my third date, as I was not interested in anyone I went to school with. He was two years older and had come back to the school for an event that I was participating in. A friend of his introduced us as he knew me because we went to church and youth group together. His father was the minister at our local church. Robert asked me out and we began dating. He was nineteen, and I was sixteen years old. I remember our first date because we used to joke about it. He took me to a fancy restaurant in the city, and me being a teenager from a small town, I did not even know what to order. He ordered fillet mignon, butterflied well done. I ordered spaghetti and meatballs. It is hilarious now, but at the time, I was very nervous. Believe it or not, we had a second date where we went dancing until late in the evening or early morning hours. We would talk for hours on the phone, his father told me that he wouldn't talk to anyone other than me. We had quickly hit it off and did everything together. The more time we spent together, the closer we became and eventually became each other's world.

After two-and-a-half years of dating, we got married and began our life together. We had three beautiful children and had a blast raising our kids. We were involved in whatever they did and supported them 100 percent. We coached, went on field trips, class mom, baked brownies and cupcakes for every bake sale and sports event, attended every game that all of our kids were in. Both of our boys were three seasoned athletes. Moriah tried tennis lessons but didn't like it. She was more interested in school activities and school government, which she excelled at.

I have told you all of that so you can understand when I tell you that I lost everything, I did. He was my world, my everything for the last thirty-seven years. We were like lone rangers when it came to having friends even as adults, we never really hung out with other couples, we were happy with each other.

It is the little things that get me now as I think of him. The way he used to make fun of me because I could never paint my nails without getting in on my fingers or my toes, when I put away the pans in the cupboard and the covers would make a racket that he would say some sarcastic remark, or when the door to the house is left open and he would yell out, "You don't live in a barn," all these things and so many more when they happen instantly I hear his voice and remember. I am beginning to laugh at the memories now, but in the beginning, I would just cry.

We were in love, "We loved and were loved," just like he told me two weeks before he passed away.

Chapter 10

Sitting in the chair in my living room almost four months after Robert had passed, a friend of Corey's walked in and began to talk to me. I was having a real bad day. I hadn't showered for a couple of days, combed my hair, put on any makeup, and I was still in my clothes that I hang around the house in. He spoke with me for approximately five minutes, then he walked out into our garage with my son, Corey, following him. They talked about me, obviously.

Corey's friend is a big guy and is a very influential military man (for that reason, I cannot share his name). He has a way about him; when he talks, people listen, I know I sure did. He marched right back into our living room, and he got into my face and spoke with a stern voice and told me, "Saturday, I will be back at 7:00 a.m. to get you, you better be dressed." I could only respond, "Okay." Corey and his friend have been going to yard sales for the past few years, and now, I was going too.

Saturday morning, I was up, dressed, and ready to go. He took me to yard sales all over the town. He didn't just take me to yard sales, he told me that I had to buy something that I could repaint or make something with. He made sure I had a project for the week, and he checked up on me too.

Corey's friend has become a very close friend of mine because of the time we spent together that summer. He didn't just come that Saturday, but he came every Saturday for the entire summer. Every week, he made sure I had another project to work on. That summer, I refinished, painted, and stenciled shelves, tables, stools, toy boxes, anything I could find. It kept me busy, it got me off my chair and out of my house. That simple act of kindness turned my life around and gave it purpose again. As we would go to yard sales, I began to talk to people again and was not so focused on myself. What he did showed kindness and poured love and purpose into my life again.

Investing in people is what God would have us do.

I began to spend more time with the Lord, and my heart began to change. My heart had been completely shattered into tiny slivers, absolutely unrecognizable. The Lord began the rebuilding process of my heart into what He wanted, for His purpose. I was spending a great deal of my day reading my Bible and praying, and my faith was growing as God was revealing things to me about myself, my relationships, my past, and my future.

Both of the pastors from our church came to visit me one day, and we sat under the big oak tree in my backyard. The tree where we used to sit on Sunday mornings in a circle with our family. I began to tell them of the things the Lord had done for me, and they left encouraged. I had not been back to church since Robert had passed, and Pastor didn't push me as I asked him at the funeral to give me some time alone, but now he said, "It is time to return to church." I continued to tell him that I had already told my family that I was going to back to church that Sunday, but none of my kids were ready yet.

I did go back to church that Sunday, and as I predicted, it was hard to face the people I hadn't seen in almost twelve months. I cried as I went in, I cried during worship, I cried as I left, I cried whenever anyone spoke with me, I cried whenever anyone hugged me. I did that week after week, until one day, I realized I didn't cry when I walked in. The next week, I didn't cry when someone spoke with me. It was gradual, but eventually, I made it through a whole service without having my mascara running down my face.

The Lord was reconstructing my heart as He continued to put me together again. The Holy Spirit was the glue that held my heart together. I started to feel stronger in my faith, and my relationship with the Lord.

He revealed to me why I had become shy and invisible. I had put Robert on a pedestal, and he had become my idol as I hid behind him and allowed him to speak for me and shield me from problems. I didn't grow because I allowed this to happen. He always told me to speak for myself, but I didn't as he was always my defender.

As I was sitting in the backyard reading my Bible one day, I read the scripture.

> "Every good thing given and every perfect gift is from above, coming down from the Father of lights, with whom there is no variation or shifting shadow" (James 1:17).

I sat there under the tree and looked at the shadow of the tree and realized a few things. The shade is bigger, more dense, and cooler the closer you are to the object.

As I sat there under the big oak tree in my backyard, God told me that He had a plan, and I have to trust Him. He didn't ask me what I thought about it, I chose to walk in faith and not to fight against it. I did, and it was the best decision of my life. He knows the whole picture, He knows all of what He has planned, I could only see my problems.

I want to share a lesson I learned through all that I have gone through. The Bible speaks about people worshiping idols, and I always thought about statues with people bowing in front of them. But an idol is anything you worship or adore, sometimes blindly but not deserving of it. The first commandment says, "I am the Lord thy God, you shall not have any strange gods (idols) before Me" (Exodus 20).

What God revealed to me was that I had idolized my husband. I was shocked when I realized that He was right. I had allowed myself to be lost. As I looked back and remembered a time when in church, the pastor had an altar call, and I looked to see out of the corner of my eye if my husband raised his hand because then, I would raise mine. I was allowing my husband to make my eternal decisions for me. He never knew it, of course, only God and I knew it.

I had allowed my title of wife and mother to define me. God was beginning to show me that my name defines me because He sees me as an individual. He sees me as Carol, His daughter.

My husband's personality was bold, loud, lively, and everyone wanted to be his friend. He would light up a room whenever he walked in it. He had a funny wit about him. When he was sick, an old friend that lives in Florida flew up to visit and told me that when they were in apprenticeship school together, everyone would try to sit next to my husband. He was like a "kingpin," and everyone wanted to be next to him. He drew them with his winning personality. Over the years, I became soft, quiet, shy, submissive, and a total wallflower. I wasn't like that as a teenager when we first met. Life had just happened, and I allowed myself to become hidden behind his personality and hidden in his shadow.

Christ doesn't want us hidden. His plan for me as His daughter was not to be hidden. I was to be actively ministering for Him. I have learned how unhealthy hiding had become. I was never unhappy, nor did I even realize what I had become!

But now, I realize that God has a bigger plan for me as I seek after Him. In my life, God has anointed my lips to speak for Him. To speak of the truths that He is showing me and revealing to me in His word. I have been saved and serving Christ for over thirty years, and I am just figuring this out. God wants and has made me to become bold. I have prayed for people in the supermarket. I have stepped out and prayed for people at the altar. I have told people that God has given me a message for them. I have learned how to listen for and hear the voice of God within my heart. He has truly blessed my life as He has taken my ashes and is making something beautiful out of them.

You see, I have shifted from being in my husband's shadow to being in Christ's shadow.

"Every good thing bestowed, and every perfect gift is from above, coming down from the Father of lights, with whom there is no variation or shifting shadow" (James 1:17).

The Father is the author of the light, His shadow never moves because He never moves. He is always the same—yesterday, today, and forever. His shadow is big enough for all of us.

Chapter 11

We had a Yorkie-Pomeranian dog which was so lovable. All twelve pounds of him. His coloring was like that of a golden retriever, that is why we chose him because he had the same coloring as Nutmeg, our Golden Retriever we had to put down. Biscotti is a lap dog, and the minute you sit, he wants to join you on your lap, because he is not allowed on the furniture, not even a paw can touch. That was the rule in our house, and he knew it. He welcomes everyone who comes in, wags his tail, and wants to be pet as well. We would tie a bandana handkerchief around his neck, and he would run and jump off our porch, and as he did, the bandana would fly like a cape over him. It was quite hilarious. He loved to chase after tennis balls as we would throw them for him, and he would play every game that the kids did.

Well, one day, he didn't look so well, and I took him to the vet which informed me that he had lymphoma and would last only about a week. I was devastated as well as my kids. I came home that day and read my Bible looking for comfort, but I was so overwhelmed I remember telling myself, "Breathe, just breathe." The feeling of life being sucked out of you at every corner is what I was experiencing. Without Robert, I had to make this decision by myself.

Saying goodbye to Biscotti was like saying goodbye to another member of our family; it was very difficult. Pets love unconditionally. Biscotti had helped us get through this past year without Robert, and now, he was the one that was sick. He was diagnosed the week before Easter. I waited until the day after Easter to return to the vet, which allowed everyone to say goodbye to Biscotti. That morning, I went alone not wanting my kids to have to go through it. I said my good-bye, gave him a hug and a kiss, then handed him to the vet. Walking out of the vet that day with tears streaming down my face and emp-ty-handed, it gave me those same feelings of being alone.

Our family has had its share of heartache this past year, but family life continues, and our family was full of drama at the time.

The day of Robert's funeral at the coalition that followed, his younger brother decided that after the years of issues he and his wife had was enough. "Life is too short," he said as he left that day. He went home and cleaned out his closet and left his wife.

His brother went to live with a friend who he had worked with and seemed happier. What we didn't realize and didn't find out until six months later was he was confirmed to have the same lung cancer that Robert had. His was stage 3 when he got diagnosed.

After a few rounds of chemotherapy, his brother seemed to be doing okay but knew his time was limited. Almost fifteen months after Robert had passed, his brother went into the hospital. I went to visit with him and was able to talk with him extensively about the Lord. He had come to church with us for a couple of years and knew the truth but had returned to his old lifestyle. That day in his hospital room, he prayed with me and asked the Lord to forgive him of all his sins.

That night, I had a dream, which is a rare occurrence. I dreamt that there was a staircase, and I could only see the bottom few steps as the rest was covered with puffy clouds. Robert was standing on the bottom step, and our eyes connected as he gave me the look that he was proud of me, and I had done the right thing. Then he winked at me, and I knew it was him. No one knew of the game him and I used to play with other. I could wink one eye then the other with no problems. I could go back-and-forth winking quickly. He used to be frustrated at me because he had a hard time winking just one eye, he never could go back-and-forth. So when he winked at me in my dream, I was assured that he was in heaven, and I had actually seen him it wasn't just my imagination.

My mother-in-law told me the next day that she had a dream that night as well. She dreamt that Robert was in a large room, and he was making furniture for babies and little children.

I know his prayer and heart was genuine because the next time I went in to see him, he told me that he swore by accident and felt all guilty inside and asked God to forgive him again. Praise the Lord. He went into hospice and passed away two weeks later on May 6th at 5:00 a.m. He passed exactly one year three months two weeks and three days after his brother, Robert.

The day my brother-in-law died, I was numb inside, felt like I had relived Robert's illness and passing all over again. I found myself crying and crying. I am sad for my niece and my in-laws as they have now buried two out of their three sons. Robert's older brother have lost both of his brothers, my kids have lost their father and now, an uncle. I have lost my husband and now, my brother-in-law.

I am glad that he is with Lord in heaven. I'm sure his brother was waiting for him as he arrived. The family has been through more pain in the past few years that we all need to all move on and begin to heal.

After the funeral, I was thanking God that Robert's brother had accepted Jesus as Savior and Lord. I was reminded of the thief on the cross who was crucified alongside of Jesus. It didn't matter that he had lived his life apart from Christ, what mattered was that in the final moments of his life, he had asked forgiveness from Christ. As Jesus died moments before Him, that man who was beside Him on the cross went into eternity with Jesus as his Savior and heaven as his home. That gave me comfort.

On the morning after his funeral, I asked God to reveal to me any emotions that I haven't dealt with yet or maybe took the easy way out. I think being "strong" was a coverup for some things as the family has leaned on me for the past couple of years.

Life is full of surprises and throws curve balls at us, but we have to learn how to maneuver through every one of them. We are never ready for what happens, it just comes ready or not. I have learned that it is how you deal with each occurrence; each tragedy is the barometer of how long it will take you to move on from it.

Chapter 12

"You have to come back" is not the thing you want to hear after you have a mammogram. Well, I did have to go back, and that started a series of events that I am going to share with you.

I went through all the normal internal questions, *What is going to happen, Am I going to die now too, Are my kids going to be orphans?* After the events of the last couple of years, no one would have blamed me, except I didn't tell anyone other than a close friend. I didn't want my kids to worry and get all depressed if it turned out the callback was for nothing.

I asked God to give me a scripture to hang on to. He led me to the book of Joshua, Chapter 1 states over and over again, "Be strong and courageous." Well, that is good and all but that also tells me that I was about to go through something I needed strength and courage for. Not funny! On the other hand, I also knew that God had my back and would deliver me through it, which gave me the strength and courage I needed to persevere.

Joshua and Caleb were faithful while growing up in Egypt and all through the wilderness that God gave them a promise. That promise was a home. Caleb chose the hill country to live in, and he had to slay the giants that lived there in order to possess it. He did, of course, with God's help.

I believed that God was going to do that for me. To slay the giants that I faced. This seemed like a mountain I could not climb alone, and God showed me at every step that He was there with me. In my heart and in my prayers, I held onto that scripture where I would say it and believed it.

Well, after the repeat mammogram, the test showed that I had a lump and two spots, one on each breast. I had to go for a sonogram; it was confirmed, but they wanted to do an MRI to get further diagnosis. I had to get an MRI with contrast, which made me sick, so I had to get someone to drive me home. At that point, I told my children. I had kept it private for two weeks and carried inside of my heart and mind.

The following week, I had an appointment with a breast surgeon who confirmed that I had a lump and two spots on my breasts. They wanted to do further testing to determine if it was cancerous or not. The surgeon ordered a 3D mammogram and another sonogram. I scheduled both tests to be done together as I had to have them done at the hospital which was in the city.

Testing day came a week later, and of course, I have been praying hard and standing on God's promise that He game me in Joshua 1:9–10, "Have I not commanded you? Be strong and courageous! Do not tremble or be dismayed, for the Lord your God is with you wherever you go." I drove to the hospital that day confident that God was with me and was going to heal me.

The first test was the 3D mammogram which went okay, but the radiologist told me the results that the lump and spots were still there on my breasts. They were able to pinpoint the exact placement of them. The radiologist said to still go through with the sonogram, which I did. As I laid on the table and the radiologist performed the sonogram, she didn't say anything, she just kept going over and over the same areas on my breasts. She told me that she needed to go get the head radiologist, her boss. She left the room for about five minutes, which is where most people would be terrified, but I used the opportunity. I laid there and prayed. I said, "God, You told me that You had my back, that You would be with me wherever I go, well, I am here right now, and I need a miracle *right now!*"

The head radiologist came and sat next to me and performed another sonogram. After she finished from what seemed like a long time to be laying on the table, she told me, "Mrs. Irace, we cannot find the lump and one of the spots." The other one is so small, and it shows no signs of cancer. Both of the radiologists just stood there and were smiling. Well, I jumped off that table so fast, and I was crying and thanking God. I told them that God had healed me.

I left the hospital that day on a cloud, higher than nine. I knew that God had heard me, was watching me, and healed me somewhere between the 3D mammogram and the two sonograms. God is so good. I had endured the six weeks of testing to hear those words and leaning on God through it all.

The breast surgeon had called to confirm the results from the radiologists but still wanted to know about the tiny spot that was left. She ordered an MRI and a biopsy.

I had begun to ask the Lord to use me in ministry. I felt that He was calling me to minister to women. I was at a Wednesday staff prayer when I felt that He told me I would be ministering to women. I literally laughed out loud, just like Sarah did when she heard she was going to have a baby at age ninety. "With my background with women, really, God? You know that I don't like them, You know all they have done to hurt me, why are You calling me to women's ministry?" God has a way like none other.

At the first MRI, I had a radiologist which was a very nice young woman. I asked her if she went to church, she told me that she used to go with her grandmother but doesn't go any longer. After sharing with her, I invited her to come with me the following Sunday. Even though she said she would come, she didn't. That day, I instantly felt a connection to her and continued to pray for her even though I knew I would probably never see her again.

When I went back to the hospital for the MRI biopsy that was ordered by the breast surgeon, wouldn't you know it, that same radiologist was there, and she came and said hello to me. I prayed and said, "Okay, Lord, make a way." I went into the room with the MRI but for some reason, they were not ready and had to set it up which would take twenty minutes. Since I had already changed into the johnny which they had given me for the biopsy, I couldn't go back into the waiting room. So that radiologist and I sat in a private room for twenty minutes. Yes, God made a way, all right. I began asking her about her life, and she was telling it all to me, she was very open as she told me that she felt she could trust me. Then, I asked her to church again, and I told her, "I am back here again just for you, please come to church because I don't want to come back again for another test." She was taken aback by my boldness but then said, "I haven't told you everything." She went on to tell me that she had never worked on that floor or even in that department, and she had never even done a biopsy before. She told me that she works on the pediatrics floor, and she had only been there in that department twice and both times she had me as a patient. Oh yeah, God was moving, big time, and I knew it. She did too because she said as I was leaving that she felt God was trying to get her attention.

After the biopsy, another nurse was in the room with me, and I was bleeding, so she had to compress my breast where they did the biopsy for ten minutes to stop the bleeding. I am sure you can guess what we spoke about, that's right, I began to ask her if she went to church. She told me that she used to go with her first husband to a local Assembly of God church, and her mother was the women's ministry head. I instantly thought to myself, *Okay, God, give me all the words she needs to hear.* She had just gotten remarried, and her new husband didn't want to go to church, but I told her to go with her mother, and her husband might follow. I also told her that I had ministered to the MRI radiologist and that she needed to go as well that it would be nice for them to go together. By the time I had left, they both hugged me and told me they would go to church. Praise God.

God will use any situation if you allow yourself to be used. He showed me that in my most embarrassing situation, He used me to minister to those women.

The results were in from the biopsy, and the breast surgeon called and asked me to come into the office to see her. My best friend accompanied me that day and was there in the office when the surgeon told me that the tiny spot left on my breast was not and never would become cancer! The surgeon hugged me as she knew the process I had been through. My friend and I were in the parking garage walking back to our cars, and we both screamed, "Thank You, Jesus." It was awesome to hear it echo within the walls of the parking garage. Anyone within hearing distance couldn't help but hear us.

I had to do follow-up mammograms and surgeon visits for the next two years, but I am cancer-free. God used this to show me that

He still heals. I had begun to doubt it as I had prayed so hard for my husband to be healed, and he wasn't. He was also showing me that He uses anyone who is willing to be used and that I could trust Him to have my back, just lean on Him.

"This hope we have as an anchor of the soul, a hope both sure and steadfast and one which enters within the veil" (Hebrews 6:19).

My anchor, the One I cling to in the middle of my storms keeps me firmly planted, steadfast, and able to stand in the middle of the water as the waves crash over my head. The waves touch me, but I will not move from that firm place. He allows me to stand, He holds me up and in place not allowing the enemy to take me away or off the path He has set my feet on. "The enemy came only to steal, kill, and destroy" (John 10:10a), especially when you become a threat. But thank God He has the final word, the only word that we should be listening to, "I came that they may have life, and have it abundantly" (John 10:10b).

An anchor can hold an entire ship, imagine what Christ as my anchor can do for me. My life has had many storms, some small, some strong. I have learned Who to hang on to, Who to attach myself to. I know that if I take my eyes off of Christ, I will attach to something or someone else. The enemy isn't an anchor, he wants to pull us away a little at a time, so we don't realize how much and how far away we really are. I have been in both places in my life.

I have been swayed away by the enemy and awoke one day and didn't realize how I got where I was and didn't know where I was or who I had become. All it took was saying, "I'm sorry, Lord, please forgive me, set my feet on the right path again." He let His light shine in my darkness, and I followed. Today, I am hanging onto Christ as I have too much to lose if I ever let go. What a privilege we have to be able to enter within the veil and have a relationship with Jesus. Think about opening the curtain in your living room and allowing others to see into your daily life, to see how you really live, to see who you really are. That is what Christ did when He allowed us to enter within His veil; He opened the curtain, and now, we can see who He really is and see Him as He moves. Praise God.

It seems in scripture that the people who went through the storms were those who were His disciples. The ones that were closest to Him. The ones He had an important task for. He knew they could handle it but also had to teach them to hang on and who they could trust and lean on. It is our choice to hang on to the anchor of our soul or let go and drown in the circumstances of life and be swept away.

God was showing and teaching me that I needed to hang on to Him. That He was my anchor and no matter what the enemy was going to throw at me, He had my back. I had just gone through a storm of incredible magnitude and came out revealing how strong my faith really was. I relied on Christ when no one else understood me or could help me. I leaned on Him when I needed reassurance, comfort, provision, mercy, and grace. He saved my soul, He healed my body, He provided all that I needed and has now called me to minister for Him. Praise His holy name.

Chapter 13

Grief is a natural part of life; it is a process that one must go through after you lose someone you love. Loving and having a relationship with someone will someday come to an end, but you will survive and learn to live again. Some are blessed to have other relationships along their journey of life.

My uncle, who has lost two wives to illness, told me after Robert had passed away that I would one day move on and desire companionship again. At that time, I said, "No way, no one could ever replace him." But about a year later, I did begin to desire companionship again. I couldn't see it at the time Robert had passed away, but as time went on, and time does continue on, my heart began to change. I found myself lonely and began to ask God to send someone to me.

I remember when Robert had just passed away, some of my first words were, "I don't want to be a widow, I don't want to be alone." It was hard for me to imagine not being connected to someone. Robert and I had been together for thirty-seven years.

Grief has many stages and emotions that need to be worked through. First, you are in disbelief that this is happening, the shock of the death of your loved one. During the week of the funeral with all the decisions and preparations, you find yourself going through the motions of "getting things done." Then, denial or hoping that it isn't true, that somehow the outcome can be reversed. This happened to me. Legal and financial matters begin to overwhelm you with the stack of papers that need to be filled out, appointments to be made and kept, phone calls, documents, life insurance policies, checking and saving accounts, IRAs, pensions, social security, credit cards, transfer of ownership of vehicles, that is just to name a few. It is overwhelming the work that needs to be done at a time in your life that you are hurting the most.

As time begins to move, you find yourself angry. You find yourself yelling at the picture of your loved one that you have been cherishing for the past couple of months. You are upset that you are left with this mess, that you are left alone, that you have to make these decisions without your spouse. If you lost someone to an accident, you begin to ask questions, was it their fault, what don't I know about the accident, what caused it, could it have been prevented? In the case of an accident. you don't usually have the opportunity to say, "Goodbye," or "I'm sorry, forgive me."

In either case, there are usually feelings or issues that are left not dealt with. Maybe an argument or words that were spoken, final words that may not have been very kind, forgiveness given or needed. The past that has crept into the present and no one to give the solution. With these emotions swirling around your mind and heart, there is no one to turn to because the one you needed to talk to had just passed away.

I found that only God knew how to handle me, could give me what I needed, and truly knew my heart even when I didn't know myself what would help. I began to spend more and more time reading my Bible, praying, and just talking with the Lord like He was sitting in the chair next to me. I needed someone to talk to, to confide in, to help make sense of what was happening. Someone that could weed through my babble, my tears, and all my emotions to truly know what I meant.

After months in this stage of grief, I began to feel peace, meaning to life again, a purpose and a reason to continue on. A longing to see what direction my life was going to head in next. I began to remember what my uncle had said to me months earlier. I was tired of the loneliness, began to desire company, companionship, someone to share things with again, someone to go to dinner with, someone to come home to, to look forward seeing at the end of the day. Someone that would make my heart beat again.

As I was taking this step towards healing, God was ministering to me like no one else could. I was spending time with the Lord,

He listened to me, to my prayers, all my requests, my comments, concerns, issues. Anything that came up in the house, the repairs, the cars, the kids, family, friends, etc. He heard everything I said and sent an answer. I began to see things just happen and knew that God was in control.

I thought of the dream that Robert's best friend had about the spiral and the flash of light then the spiral reversed direction. We always thought that it was for Robert that he would be healed, and life would continue. But that was not the case, after the flash of light, where Robert went to heaven, and my life had reversed direction or gone into a new direction.

In the second chapter of Joshua, we meet Rahab. She was a woman that hid the spies that Joshua had sent out to investigate the city of Jericho. The Bible doesn't specify why they went to her and not to someone else. The guards that were protecting her city were looking for the men, and she hid them in her home and risked the life of herself and her family. They promised to protect her when they returned with the army to attack her city. Obviously, it was ordained for them to go to Rahab because God had a plan for her life. She had no idea what was about to happen. God has a plan for each of us; we don't know what it is, but He is always working "behind the scenes" until one day, it all makes sense. For me, I had met people that I needed for this time in my life to figure things out concerning my home, finances, etc. I realized that the way I had met these people was a divine appointment arranged by God beforehand. Why would I ever doubt that He is caring for me and arranging things for my future. If He took care of my past and my present, then I know that He has my future all taken care of too. God is always the same, yesterday, today, and forever. He is not a respecter of person, if He did it for me, then He will do it for you as well.

The men lodged there, they stayed in her home until it was safe for them to leave. She was an innkeeper; her home was the place where people came to stay if they were just visiting the city. She had asked for forgiveness from her former life as she was a prostitute. "In the same way, was not even Rahab the prostitute also justified by works when she received the messengers and sent them out by another way" (James 2:25)? It was a good work. She did it by faith which shows that she had put her evil deeds away. She didn't fear man, she feared God. She could have been killed for defying her own city as they were at war. She lied to protect them which shows that she wasn't familiar with the laws of God. She knew her lifestyle was wrong and wanted to change. Isn't that where we all started, realizing that one day, our life is not where we thought it was going to be?

God had a plan for Rahab; she was to be part of the bloodline of Jesus. She was a prostitute and a sinner like the rest of us. He can take the worst of sinners and have a purpose for them. He is even willing to have them as part of His own family. If He can accept them, we should too.

They came to Rahab in secret, she hid them, she lied for them, she made them promise her if she helped them that they would protect her. Secretly, they were sent out by Joshua to spy on Jericho, but they were seen. Things done in secret do become known. She also knew and heard about God, verse 11, and she confessed to God her sins.

They kept their promise to her. When the walls fell down, her part of the wall remained. When life around us is collapsing or weakening, if we cry out to the Lord, He will be faithful and save us even if our life is crumbling like Rahab. He will keep us from falling. He will be our strong tower and our strength. He is faithful.

They made an exchange that night—a life for a life. Isn't that what God did for us. No wonder she is in God's bloodline, she gave mercy and received mercy.

The next person you share with may be the next Rahab. They may not look like it but may be an important person in God's family. I don't believe there are coincidences in God, He has planned it all.

When Robert's friend brought us to the Lord, he didn't know that one day, we would be youth pastors and touch hundreds or thousands of teenagers' lives, or pre-marriage counselors to help couples have the best start to their life together, or board members that would be making major decisions for our church.

The teens we ministered to became pastors where some are living around the world, missionaries, political officials, ministerial district pastors, lawyers, doctors, soldiers, truck drivers, chefs, professional wrestler, the impact ripples because of the teens are now grown with families of the own. We taught them about Christ, but we also showed them how to be good husbands, wives, fathers, and mothers. Many came from single parent homes, inner-city households, or dysfunctional families in some way. I know we made a difference because many of them have called, written, or have come by to see me this past couple of years.

I began to heal by spending time with God, and He revealed things to me, about me, in His word and about people who are hurting. Maybe God has revealed these things to you, but to me, this was new at that moment in time. The word is alive and active meaning that for any given moment, God has the answers we need. The word goes into the depths of our heart, our thoughts, our situation, and begins to heal, if we allow it to. I allowed it as I began to heal.

Chapter 14

The first-year anniversary of Robert's passing was quickly approaching, and I was beginning to feel like there was new life ahead for me. I had asked the Lord about removing my rings, so I had that hope in my heart that He had something more for me. Don't misunderstand me, the day I removed my rings, I hesitated and cried and cried. I couldn't believe that I was no longer married to Robert. It was the final step of saying goodbye, the end of our marriage vows, and one more tear in my heart. Even though I had made the decision to "move on," my heart was anything but healed.

My heart through this whole year had been torn into little pieces, crumbled, and smashed like someone had stepped on them. Even when I felt a little piece make its way back, something always came up to remove it again. Only God could give me new life. Only God could give me a new heart.

"But now, O Lord, You are our Father; we are the clay, and You are the potter, we are all the work of Your hand" (Isaiah 64:8).

"The vessel that He was making of clay was spoiled in the hand of the potter; so He remade it into another vessel, as it pleased the potter to make" (Jeremiah 18:4).

God was remaking my heart and my life into something that was useful for His purpose. Not that it wasn't useful before, but that season of my life was over, and He was directing me on a new journey. At times, I felt like another piece was put into place, and all I could do was thank God for not leaving me the way I was.

One particular Sunday morning, as I was driving to church, I asked God, "Please let me know if there is someone else for me?" As I was approaching the traffic light in front of a shopping commons in a neighboring town, the light was turning red, and I was stopping when a car pulled in front of me. I would have been upset had I not seen the license plate on the car. It was as if God placed His answer right in front of me. The license plate read: 808 YUP. I quickly grabbed my cell phone and took a picture of it because I knew people would think I was crazy. Remember "808" was my husband's nickname and how whenever I see it, I think of him. God was letting me know that He not only heard my question but was answering it, and He answered it right away. Thank You, Jesus.

A friend of mine in church had lost her husband about eight months after I lost Robert. We were talking about removing our wedding rings, and I told her what happened to me and that I decided to wait until the one-year anniversary. She said it made sense that we wait until we had lived through all four seasons with all the holidays and special events in each one. I had explained how living in New England has four very different seasons, and we enjoyed each one as a couple and as a family.

As part of our church community, we have "small groups." They are small groups of people that meet monthly in someone's home or in a specific place to get together and talk, share the Word of God, and build relationships. I was not part of a small group, and God had put it on my heart to join one called the "Lord's H'Art." It was an art small group. I figured since I was an interior designer, that I would have something in common with some of the other people. I didn't realize that we would be painting. I cannot paint or draw, but that is what we did and had a good time doing it. Well, that first night that I went, I was uneasy and not sure that I really wanted to do this, so I was outside in the hallway pacing back-and-forth several times. Eventually, I made the decision to go in.

The leader of the small group was an artist, and I only knew a few of the people in the group. The leader stood up in front of the room and began to describe what we would be doing that evening in our group. She said we are going to paint a picture of the "four seasons." As soon as I heard that, I threw up my hands into the air and said, "Okay, God, I know that you want me here for a reason, I give up running, use me for Your purpose." It is awesome when God arranges for things to happen to get your attention. Well, He sure got mine that night.

In that group, I made more friends and had the opportunity to minister to most of them as they were new in the church. I went there thinking I was going to receive, but I ended up giving, and it felt good to give of myself again. God was opening my heart to minister to these women.

During my prayer time, I asked my heavenly Father to arrange a marriage for me, as fathers did in the Old Testament, they chose a mate for their daughters. I asked God to choose for me, that He knew what I needed, who I needed, and who needed me. The desire to be with a man again began to grow and grow inside of me. The feelings of loneliness had long set in, and I was longing for a man's touch and intimacy. I desired the kindred spirit, the best-friend relationship with a man, to love, touch, hold, share my life with, to encourage and support each other. I asked my Father to write a love story in heaven for me.

I told Him, "I only go to a couple places regularly, church and the market. You have to have him meet me there." What I didn't realize at the time was that I had put God in a box and told Him what I thought again. He does not need any suggestions from me. Trust me.

My church has three weekend services because of the amount of people that attend. This particular Saturday night service, I was there praying before service, and God gave me a vision of me standing on the altar in a wedding gown, the gown had straps and was simple but elegant. That vision was a promise that I was holding on to for the Lord knew how much I wanted to meet someone and get remarried.

I questioned the Lord as to where the groom was, and the Lord told me that he wasn't ready yet. That he was only a couple steps away. Let me tell you, those couple steps seemed to take an eternity. When you are waiting for something to happen, it never seems like it is quick enough, but it ends up being in God's perfect timing.

I woke up praying for Kindred Spirit 2, Robert was 1. Praying for him and his children, that the Lord would make them ready and for my kids as well. I asked the Lord to have him stand in front of me and ask me out for a cup of coffee. I desire someone to love and be loved again. Someone who doesn't mind all my flaws especially as I am getting older.

I prayed for a godly man, who loves the Lord above all else, who would worship standing next to me at the altar, handsome, have hair—I am not into the new bald look, I like to play with hair—be strong, have eyes only for me, romantic, hard worker, kindred spirit, encourager, make me laugh, appreciative, thankful, desirous, passionate, compassionate, and so much more.

One day, I sat down and truly began to think about what I would want in a husband. I made a list, yes, I made a list, don't judge me. I took out a legal pad and began to write a very detailed list of what I thought I would like. Did I say it was detailed, it really was. I wrote three full pages of that legal-sized pad and then ripped it out as I was going to keep it tucked away. But I felt guilty that I had made it, so I ripped it up and threw it in the trash and apologized to God. I told Him, "You know the perfect man for me, You are my Father, You arrange it for me."

I went to coffee with a dear friend of mine who is a minister. She was telling me that she had just gone to a conference the week before, and she had prayed with a woman, and God told her a name of a person for her future. I had never experienced anything with that much detail. I went home that night and prayed that I wanted a name of my future husband.

I had a dream that night, which is rare, and woke up knowing the name of my husband and even his nickname. I told all three of my kids, my best friend, another close friend, plus I wrote it in my journal. I told my pastor but would not tell him the name because I didn't want him to set me up. His name is Richard, and his nickname was Rich, but some call him Rick. Which seemed odd to me because my father-in-law's name is Richard, and his nickname is Dick.

As time went on and I didn't meet anyone, I began looking at every man who came into church, at every man in the grocery store, at the deli counter, and sad to say that not one even piqued my interest. In July, our church holds a weeklong VBS, Vacation Bible School, for the kids in our church and surrounding neighborhood children. As a result of VBS, we don't have midweek Bible study that particular week. I figured that I would go check out the men at a friend's church. I was trying to help God. Wrong!

I looked around before and after service, not one for me. So I left the church parking lot and took a right hand turn, and the traffic light was only approximately two hundred feet from the church parking lot, and a car hit the bumper on my car. I had gotten out and spoken to the woman who hit my car then called the police, but she took off and left me holding the price tag for fixing my car. I instantly felt in my heart that I had made a mistake, and I was searching someplace that I shouldn't have. I was wrong, and it cost me seven hundred dollars. God let me know that I had to pay for my mistake. He reminded me what I told Him, that I only go to church and the market.

A month later, my parents had decided to help out me and my brother. They had decided they were going to bless us and have our driveways paved. My brother and I share a driveway as we live next door to my parents. My father saw a neighbor was having his driveway done, and he went to speak to the owner of the company that was paving their driveway and asked him to come give us a price as well. My father had gotten two different prices from two companies but felt this particular company was better suited for our job.

My father had arranged everything with this paving company. On the edge of the top of my driveway, there was a large pine tree that Robert had cut down, and the stump was still there. I had requested that they remove the stump with their equipment while they were grading the driveway. The day they were scheduled to begin working on our driveway, I couldn't leave because I wanted to make sure that they removed the stump that I had mentioned to the owner of the company when he priced it out for my father. As I was waiting for them to show up with all their equipment and begin the job, I was doing morning devotions.

When I was finished with my devotions, I went onto my Facebook and did one of those things where you put in your name, and it connects you to something. Mine happened to be a scripture. The scripture was Isaiah 58:11: "The Lord will guide you always, He will satisfy your needs in a sun-scorched land and will strengthen your frame. You will be like a well-watered garden, like a spring whose waters never fail."

The post that came up had my picture and Isaiah 58:11 in a box and Psalm 23 on the bottom half of the screen.

"The Lord is my Shepherd, I shall not want, He makes me lie down in green pastures. He leads me beside still waters. He restores my soul. He leads me in paths of righteousness for His name's sake. Even though I walk through the valley of the shadow of death, I will fear no evil, for you are with me; Your rod and Your staff, they comfort me."

I wrote something as I posted this on my account. It was 9:59 a.m.

My post was telling about being youth pastors with my husband and how we always participated in youth choirs. One year, when we did a church-wide missions play and the youth performed a couple of songs, and as part of the song, there were some speaking spots. I had to recite a scripture and mine was this particular scripture in Isaiah. Coincidence, not in God.

As soon as I posted this, I began to hear the rumble of paving equipment outside my door. I went outside and began to take photos of the beginning of the process. I instantly reminded the owner of the stump he had promised to remove before paving over that section. He had his men come up our very long driveway, and they began the process of removing the stump, but what they revealed was three very large stones underneath. They had to be removed as well so the pavement wouldn't heave in the cold weather.

I began talking with one of the men who were helping them to remove the stones. As we were waiting for a piece of equipment to arrive, we began talking about my yard, my brother's yard, our long driveways, stuff like that. As they were there working on those stones for a while, we spoke on and off. I asked about his family, he told me he had three sisters, I told him I had two sisters and a brother. My father was there, and we began talking about Florida as my parents spend time there. Our eyes had met on a couple occasions, and we were both attracted I could tell. He was all sweaty as it was August, and he was working hard to dig out the large stones and digging a trench to bury wire for light posts that I have going down my driveway.

At lunchtime, I was walking away to go inside while they ate their lunch in the shade, one of the men he worked with called out to him, "Hey, Rick, come over here." I instantly turned around and stared at him, and I knew that God had made a connection.

The next day, I didn't see him as he was driving the trucks full of hot asphalt. By the end of the third day, they had finished the job, and I was sitting inside as that man, Rick, was not there at all that day. He came to load the equipment and had walked up to the top of my driveway and began talking to the men, when I heard his voice, I ran outside and to say hello.

Both of my parents were there as we checked everything out to make sure it was a good job before they paid the owner. My parents, myself, and Rick walked down the driveway, and as I stood there with my parents, he just waved and got in his truck and drove away. While we were still there, he turned around and drove back again waving at me.

A couple days had gone by, and I was outside washing my car and weeding my flower gardens when I began to ask God, "How will I ever know if that was the right man or not, I have no way of ever seeing him again." A half-hour went by and a car drove up the driveway, Massachusetts plates, gold SUV, I don't know anyone with that car. There was someone at my front door, but I was in the garage vacuuming my car. I walked outside in my old work clothes and guess who was there, *yup*, it was Rick.

We stood there on my brick walkway between two pillars for about an hour. The very first question that I asked him was, "Do you go to church?" He said not presently, but he believed in God. I thought to myself, God how can this be, You bring me a man but he is not a believer. I can't do it. I can't fall in love and marry a man who doesn't love the Lord. He is not the right one. After the hour of talking, he walked over to his car to leave and asked me to go for a cup of coffee. I just stood there. I know what I had told God. I could feel my heart beating very fast, but I wasn't sure and didn't want to make a mistake. "I'm not ready, but I'll think about it," I told him.

He gave me his number and asked me to call him. He asked me what my name was, and I told him, then I asked him what his was, and he said, "My name is Richard, my nickname is Rich, but the guys from the paving company call me Rick." After hearing that, my heart was beating very quickly, but I acted all cool and collected.

I did call him a few days later and reiterated that I was not ready to date. He said, "Let's just meet for a cup of coffee." He called me on and off for a couple of weeks, and we talked for like an hour every time he called. I actually found myself smiling whenever I heard his voice. I was very confused, I seemed to enjoy his conversation, I was physically attracted to him, but he didn't go to church, which was number one on my list.

"God, what do I do?" I was praying.

By the way, God blessed me with a female best friend for the first time in my life, and she has walked through this past year with me. I have told her about my dreams, my vision, meeting Richard, and she is excited for me and continues to pray that I would know God's will.

Chapter 15

After a couple of weeks of talking on the phone, I agreed to go for a cup of coffee. My eldest son was not happy with me meeting with this man. I told him that I was going to share the gospel with him. Personally, I needed to know. I needed to know if he is the one that God sent for me. If God did send him, then who am I to say no.

That next weekend, we met for a cup of coffee. He had a bouquet of flowers for me, which made me feel really uncomfortable, like he was trying too hard. We sat outside and talked for a couple of hours, we talked about our families, jobs, children, surface topics. I shared the Lord with him, and he told me that he used to go to church as a kid and raised his family in the church. That he believed in God but did not know Him like I seemed to. He told me that he was a truck driver and would talk to God all the time as if He was sitting there in the truck with him. I felt bad that I had judged him so quickly. He was a very nice man, and I was very attracted.

As we were walking to our cars after our first date, he gave me the flowers, and I just said thank you and walked away. I wanted to kiss him, and I knew that he wanted to kiss me. As I drove away, I told the Lord, "I shared the gospel with him, but where is this going, does he want a relationship with You?"

He called me the following week, but I had a prior engagement, so I told him that I would call him when I was finished. I got done early enough that we could meet for dinner. We had such a wonderful time at dinner, and a few times, he had reached over the table and touched my arm and wanted to hold my hand. I thought that it was odd, but it was very gentle and genuine. We talked for a few hours there in the restaurant and had a nice meal, but when he walked out to our cars, it was different this time. Something had stirred within me that I didn't see coming. I felt like a freight train was going to burst out of me.

He walked me to my car, and he leaned in to kiss my cheek, but when I leaned over, our lips touched. I have heard the expression of fireworks and thought really. Well, let me tell you, our first kiss, right there in the parking lot was explosive. I had not kissed a man for a couple of years and didn't think I even remembered how. It's like riding a bike.

I had gone back to look at the photos I had taken on the day we met, and just seventeen minutes earlier, I had posted on Facebook that God had given me a scripture that was true of my life. I began to think if I hadn't stayed home that day, if I hadn't walked outside to see what was going on, if I didn't stay and talk with Richard, how would we have ever met. I realized that the box I had put God in was so wrong. My heavenly Father had my earthly father hire this particular company where this man worked, and he comes right up and knocked on my front door and ask me out for a cup of coffee. If that isn't a love story written in heaven, then I don't know what is. I knew after only a couple times of going out with him that we were meant to be together.

The moment that Richard and I met at the top of my driveway, I'm sure all of heaven was watching. I call it our "meet and greet."

I know that God had blessed my journey and my waiting upon Him to answer my prayers. Allow yourself to be encouraged if you are asking God for something specific. Don't stop asking, don't stop pursuing because your blessing, your answer may be only seventeen minutes away.

Richard had told me that he only worked at that company as a favor to his friend. He only worked with them for seven weeks. That particular morning, he was not even going to come to my job as he hated driving the paving trucks. He said that he felt that something or someone actually picked him up and put him in the truck. Now, he knows why. He has thought, what would have happened if I didn't go that day? By the way, that was the last week he was with that company.

My children had a hard time accepting that I was dating some-one. It didn't make any difference who he was or what he was like, he just wasn't their father. The following Sunday, Richard met me at church where he gave his life to the Lord and asked Him to be his Savior. He has been coming ever since and stands right next to me during every worship service and sings with me. That was on my list. God is so good. He knows what each one of His children needs, and He provides. If we are obedient and faithful, then we receive His favor and blessings.

He met my in-laws, Robert's parents, they loved him instantly and knew he was a nice guy. They welcomed him into the family and made him feel like a part of it. My best friend was extremely happy for me, she was cautious but happy. Another close friend was happy but kept asking me questions to see if this was real. She felt it was too soon, and she didn't like it that he wasn't a Christian as long as I had been. I appreciated her concern but assured her that when she met him that she would like him. Side note: When she met him, she did like him, and they are good friends today.

He wasn't working steady at the time we started dating so we spent full days together getting to know each other. We would go away on day trips to states that are three hours away and still be talking when we got back to my house. We would sit in the driveway until midnight because we weren't done talking. My son would begin to put the outside lights on, flash the lights. It was comical because that is what we used to do to them, he is now doing to me, his mother. We obviously enjoyed each other's company very much. We discovered that we had so much in common. Instead of opposites attracting, we were both alike, and we attracted like magnets. We realized that at this stage of our life that we wanted someone who enjoyed the same things the other did.

Every Sunday after church, we would go for coffee and a bagel at a local coffee shop, but this one Sunday, we were heading in a different direction and went to a new shop. It was a very cold and windy day, and as we were walking into this particular coffee shop, I noticed an older woman sitting at a table reading a book by herself. She had chosen the best table because it had the sunshine coming through the windows and warmed that little section of the coffee shop. After we had ordered our coffee and bagel, we went to find a table to sit down and eat. As we were walking, by I stopped by this woman's table and mentioned to her that she had chosen the warmest table, and I asked her why she was there all alone. She responded to me by telling me that her husband was dying from COPD and that the nurses were at home with him. She began to tell me that she comes there every day for one hour, that is how she gets her alone time and gets to relax.

I could see that this woman was struggling with her husband's illness, so I sat down at her table and began to talk with her. I told her my story of how I had lost my husband and how my faith in Jesus carried me through the tough times. She listened intently but didn't say very much, so I just got up and went to the table that Richard had found for us to sit at. He was expecting a phone call but left his phone in his car, so he went outside for a moment to get his phone then ran back inside because it was so cold outside.

The woman that I had stopped and spoken with got up from her table and came and sat with me in the back of the coffee shop. She had thought about all that I said, and she began to tell me that she used to go to a local church but hasn't gone since her husband had gotten sick, and she really missed going. I told her that God understood and that she could pray at home because it is our hearts that matter. I asked her if I could pray for her, and she excitedly said, "Yes, please." I held her hand and prayed for her. As Richard had come back in and saw what was happening, he just held his distance until I was done praying.

The woman told me that she would never forget me because my name was Carol, and I would always be her Christmas Carol. She told me her name, and I told her that I would continue to pray for her, which I have. She told me to remember her by the Christmas song, "Feliz Navidad," as it rhymes with her name. Every time I hear that song, I think of her and lift up a prayer.

Richard and I finished our coffee and bagel and made it back through the cold to his car. As we were getting back inside, he asked me what that was all about as he didn't want to ask me, so she could hear. I told him the whole story. He loved watching the way I shared my faith, my boldness, and the way I truly cared for other people. I told him that she gave me a way of remembering her name and how she was going to remember me.

What happened next neither one of us saw it coming. I had told him a great deal about Robert and our relationship, but I had never mentioned the "808" story. It had never come up maybe because the Christmas season had not started yet. I began to explain it to him how whenever I see 808 on the clock, on an address, a license plate, etc. that I instantly think of Robert and say, "Hello," or "I love you, honey," or something along those lines. He told me that in the last eight to nine months, he has seen one particular number. He told me that it keeps coming up. He said he was at the bank and it came up. He saw it on his mother's stove. He saw it on a clock. He said it became so noticeable that he had showed his mother and best friend whenever it happened when they were with him. He never knew what it meant, and it was puzzling him.

I told him that I thought that was cool and told him that it must mean something, and one day, he will know what it means. I asked him, "What is the number?"

He said, "10:10."

When he said, "10:10," I felt the air come out of my lungs, and I needed to open the car door for air instantly. He asked me, "What is the matter?"

I responded to him that "I know what it means."

Many years earlier, like twenty or so, Robert and I had heard a message about John 10:10, and every time we saw it on the clock. we would recite it together.

"The thief comes only to steal, kill, and destroy; but I have come that you may have life and have it abundantly" (John 10:10). My kids grew up hearing the both of us reciting this, so when he passed away and it came time to pick out his cemetery memorial stone I wanted to put a scripture on it and the kids said, "Mom, it has to be John 10:10." So I had John 10:10b engraved on his memorial stone.

When I told that to Richard, his face turned white as a ghost, and we had a God moment right there in his car in the parking lot of the coffee shop. *Wow*! At that very moment, we both knew that God had something for us, that God was definitely the One who put us together. It instantly erased any doubt that I had, that my friend tried to instill in me, that might have been in the back of my mind about his newness to the Lord. I knew in that moment that God was in this relationship, and He had put His stamp of approval on it.

Richard had never experienced anything like this before and was completely shaken by it. I told him that is how God moves and lets us know it is His will.

As I thought about how long he had been seeing 10:10 was eight to nine months, that was about the same time that God had answered me with the license plate, 808-YUP. God is so good. He certainly has written our love story in heaven.

Chapter 16

We were not even engaged yet, we didn't have a wedding date, but I woke up one morning at 5:05 a.m. Then the next morning, I woke up at 5:05 a.m. It caught my attention, and I asked God what it meant, thinking He wanted me to pray for something, but He shocked me and said, "That was your wedding date." I jumped out of bed and was excited, shocked but excited.

We had only been dating for four months. I told Richard, and he was excited. We had talked about getting married, but we didn't think that soon. I know that sounds crazy, but we just knew it was right.

When we went to pick out my engagement ring, we had both looked at every ring in the store and nothing seemed right. The man helping us said, "I have one I think you will like, we haven't put it out yet because it is new." It was the one. The minute I put it on, we both knew it was the right one. The man went on to tell us that there was not another like it, that there were three small stones along both sides of the diamond, and they represented the past, present, and future. It sealed the deal as we were joining lives and families.

When Moriah had gotten married a few years earlier, the altar had been renovated, and there was no center steps for the bride and groom, so Robert had decided to make a set of steps. We purchased the wood, and he constructed the steps that are now part of the altar at our church.

As I sat in church that next week, I was looking at the altar and became emotional as I realized that Robert had built them for Moriah, but now, I was also going to be using them. To think that my first husband made the steps that I would stand on to marry my second husband. *Wow!*

We traveled to Florida to visit my parents, and the night before we left, Richard knelt in front of me and asked me to marry him. He was very emotional and serious because he loved me so much. He never intended to remarry, but God had changed his heart. Of course, I said, "Yes!" We went to Florida the next morning but didn't tell our children until we returned that we were engaged even though they knew we had a wedding date.

Leading up to the wedding was not easy. My children were not happy, and they let me know. I had met Richard's two sons as well as his daughter-in-law and their baby. His kids were happy for him as he had been divorced for a few years. His daughter lived in Texas, so I didn't get to meet her until the wedding reception. She was very bubbly and personable.

My daughter, Moriah, who was six months pregnant, stood up for me and his youngest son stood up for him. Corey walked me down the aisle, which I know was very difficult for him.

When I walked into the church that day, I looked forward and stared at Richard and didn't look at anyone else, I couldn't or else I would have broken down and cried. I recited my vows to Richard with boldness and sureness. I knew he was the one God had sent for me.

So, we met in August, started dating in September, were engaged in January, and we got married in May. What a roller coaster of a relationship. With God, all things are possible. I totally understand that it seems crazy, but we just knew it was right and it was God.

I said all of that because I know that children don't see their parents as people with feelings. They just see Mom and Dad. I kept telling them that I am a woman with feelings and emotions too, and I want to share them with someone. I was ready for the next leg of my journey, but my children were not at all ready to see me with another man.

Richard and I had an incredible honeymoon in Aruba. And it took a few weeks for us to move everything of his into our home and begin the process of combining lives.

Together we have six children, two grandchildren, a son-in-law, and a daughter-in-law. We have three sets of parents as Robert's parents have become a second set of parents to me as we have become very close since Robert passed away. They are truly happy for both of us. Richard's mother and stepfather—Richard's father passed away from cancer as well—they have welcomed me into their family with open arms.

Both of my boys still live at home with Richard and I, and it has been an adjustment for all of us, but they have gotten used to him being there. Corey even said a few months ago that he can see that Richard was the right choice for me and my family. That was huge for him to say.

Chapter 17

Our granddaughter was turning one and her dad and mom threw her a big backyard birthday party. This was only the third time that I had gotten together with Richard's oldest son, and when we left that day, he came over to me and hugged and kissed me twice. He told me that he loved me. From what I hear, that is so unlike him, but from the beginning, it seemed that we had hit it off. So I left that day with a huge smile on my face knowing that he had accepted me into his family as his stepmom, and he knew his dad was truly happy.

Seven weeks after our wedding, while I was out running errands, I had a phone call that no parent ever wants to receive. Richard's youngest son was calling me trying to get a hold of Richard. Richard's oldest son was killed in a motorcycle accident the night before, and no one saw him until the following morning. I had to call Richard and tell him that his first-born son had been killed. You cannot imagine how I felt telling him that. All he could do was scream and cry. He kept screaming, "No, no, no..."

He came home from work that day and picked me up, and we drove to his son's house. We didn't know all the details of the accident, and there were many questions that still haven't been answered. Everyone in the family and close friends had gathered to offer support. Richard's son was thirty-four years old and left his wife and one-year-old daughter.

After the week of the funeral and the shock of losing a child, Richard had changed. Richard has questions about the accident, about how his son died, why didn't anyone stop to help, etc.

I began to ask God, "Why? Why did You put us together, just to rip us apart, how can I be going through this again? Why after only seven weeks of wedding bliss did this have to happen?" I never asked

God why when Robert had died figuring that there was a reason, but this relationship was just so new, I began to have the questions.

Again, there are no answers to any of these questions. Richard has suffered incredibly over the loss of his son. He holds every memory dear, and he latches onto anything he can get that belonged to him. Richard who was so happy, funny, and made me laugh again, the storyteller, personable to everyone he met was now miserable, quiet, sad, and angry; something inside of him died. His son who was most like him as they had the same interests and similar jobs. So Richard feels like he lost the one who understood him when no one else did.

Months later, we went to Florida again to see my parents and upon our trip home, something strange happened. We were going through security at the Fort Myers Airport, and Richard's stuff had gone through quickly, and he was putting his shoes and belt back on when mine was taking an incredibly long time to process. I even said, "What is taking so long?" When out of nowhere, a woman came over and stood next to me and began to tell me that she had noticed both of us and how happy we seemed together and how Richard never took his eyes off of me. She began to tell me that she was a widow, and it has been real hard. I began to minister to her and told it would get easier with the passing of time. My things came through and the guard told me to move along, and as I did, I turned around to say something else to the woman, but I could not find her anywhere. Richard, who was constantly watching me never saw her. It was as if she was an angel sent for me to open my mouth and minister in the strangest places.

A couple months after that, Richard and I were in the supermarket, and I was standing at the deli counter, and a woman came up behind me and said that she had been watching both of us and noticed how much our love just glowed. As I stood there, the Lord told me to minister to her, but I didn't know what to say until I turned to look at her and saw her wearing an oxygen mask. Of course, I had to say something. I asked her, "Why are you wearing the oxygen mask?" She went on to tell me that her husband died from COPD, and her son is afraid of losing her too so wants her on oxygen. I ministered to her as a widow and asked her if I could pray for her. I stood there proud as could be at that deli counter and prayed for that woman.

In Joshua 4, when the Israelites had approached the Jordan River, God told Joshua to have the priests carrying the ark go first into the river. Once they were in the water, it stopped flowing just like the Red Sea did for Moses. The Israelites walked through on dry ground, not mud, not wet or damp, but dry. When God does something, He does it completely. He made a way for them to cross. When they got safely to the other side, God told Joshua to have one man from each tribe go to the middle of the river where the priests were standing and get a stone and put it on their shoulder and carry it to where they were lodging. Those stones were memorial stones for them to remember.

Why didn't God have them grab a stone while they were walking across the river? Why did He wait until they had completely crossed? Because God didn't want them to choose just any stone. He wanted them to finish their journey across the Jordan so they would remember that they had crossed it and that God would help them again in the future when they needed Him. God wanted them to look back and know that they made it through, just like the storm my kids and I went through, we can all look back and know that we made it.

They had to go back to the middle where the priests were holding the ark and get their stone, a big one, a boulder—they had to put it on their shoulder which means it was heavy. God wants us to look back to the middle of our storm, where it was the most turbulent, when it seems that we would never reach the other side and see that God was there with us all along. To go back to the middle and gather a boulder, big enough, heavy enough that we would remember carrying it out! That we will remember that God was with us through the storm, and He will be there through the next one.

The ark which represents God's presence was in the middle of the river. Not moving, just standing there until we made it all the way across. God wasn't moving, God doesn't move, He is always the same. The middle of our storm is the darkest, the deepest water; when we feel like we could drown or feel like giving up, He gives us the strength to continue on. He is there for us to lean on, to depend on, to give us that boost we need when we are deep into the waters, and it is just as far to go back as it is to go forward.

When you look back over your life, you can see all the memorial stones as well. Knowing that He brought you through many storms and was faithful every time. You can even see how straight your path has been, or where you went off course, and He had to guide you back. Sometimes, the storm is what brings us to the other side where we get back on the correct path for our life.

He said to pile them where they lodged that night. At that point in their life they left the marker—the memorial stone—they didn't stay there. They continued their journey. Your journey your life doesn't end after the storm, and it doesn't stay in the same place. If you are still looking at a memorial stone, you haven't moved on. You must get your feet moving again. God has bigger plans for you.

The stones in the middle were also smoother as they had been beaten by the water the most. The seasons in our life, the trials we go through can smooth out the rough spots in us, if like these stones we trust in God to get us through.

God sent the priests into the water first because God has already been where we are going. He goes before us. He leads the way. He prepares the path for us to walk on.

God then had Joshua put twelve stones in the middle of the Jordan. He was marking the middle of the water, the place where they crossed as God was there with them. Then, the water came over the banks again, back to normal. The stones are still there, whether we see them or not, they are still there. The experience was real, the hard season was real, God is real. Life goes on, it doesn't stop because of one trial or rough time in our life. By putting stones in the middle, those stones will now become smooth as they are beaten by the water.

The priests and the ark came out of the Jordan. God is on the move. He didn't stay there. If you are through your storm, why would you want to stay there? You want Him to go before you to the next one. That is exactly what He did for the Israelites, and He does for us.

They came out in battle array, they came out ready for battle, dressed and strengthened. You may be weary from the journey that you have been on, but gather your strength, put on the armor of God and get ready for battle because the enemy is always looking for someone to take down.

As a widow myself for a little over three years, I can testify that becoming a widow and living through it was the hardest storm I have ever been through. I made it, praise God. I made it only because I leaned on Jesus and allowed Him to guide me through it. He has strengthened me in the areas that I was weak in and taught me lessons that I will never forget. He allowed me to wallow in my grief for a short time but had me moving again through life. The anniversary of your loved ones' death will always be a difficult day as you remember where you were and the events that happened on that day. As the years begin to go by, I have found each one to be a little easier.

Time continues to move as we cannot stop it or slow it down. Life continues to move. Whether you find yourself in a new relationship, spending time with your family, traveling, volunteering, or whatever makes you happy, you must take the steps to live the rest of your life. Your life is a gift from God, and your loved one that has passed would not want you to be stuck or unhappy. Live your life. You have permission to live it, you have my blessing and the blessing of your family and friends to live the life God has given to you.

God has begun to show me that I am being used with other widows and other women, especially those that are hurting. He has showed me that I will be helping to piece them back together for Him. As I have compassion for those that are hurting and understand their pain.

As I am writing this, my parents' best friend passed away, and his funeral was on Saturday. My mother-in-law, Robert's mom passed away on Sunday from Lymphoma. She was diagnosed only five weeks earlier. Her funeral was on Thursday, and the following Tuesday was Richard's son one-year anniversary.

So you can see that our first year of marriage wasn't anything like we had planned. Despite all of our loss, our love has grown, we have hung onto each other in such deep ways that most can't understand or comprehend. People that have seen all that our families have gone through cannot believe that we are still standing. It is our faith in Jesus Christ that has gotten us through. It has made us strong, and we know Whom it is Who loves us and Who we love. We serve a mighty God, and He will get us through this as He has in the past. He is the same yesterday, today, and forever.

I am presently sharing Bible studies with the women at my church on Tuesday evenings. The Lord continues to speak to me and show me that there is more for me to do in the future. He is not done with me yet.

Richard and I are looking forward to the future together. We have talked about future trips we would like to take, plans about doing something around the house, retirement, and spending more time together. We have both envisioned us together in the rocking chairs as we grow old. The love that we share has been tried through the storms of life in only a short amount of time, but we know that we can depend on each other and the Lord.

I want to thank you for taking this journey with me. I have been very transparent and real with you. I pray that you feel encouraged and hopeful about your life and that the Lord knows what is best for each of us.

If you do not have a personal relationship with the Lord, I would admonish you to simply ask Him to forgive all your sins and come into your heart. He will reveal Himself to you as you begin to walk in this new relationship with Jesus Christ as your Savior and Lord. Amen.

Thank you, and God bless you.

About the Author

In the northern hills of Rhode Island, Carol Irace-Brunetti lives with her family, along with her love of old books and her early-American style design. She loves spending time with her family, tending to her flower gardens, and sitting on the porch that overlooks her backyard. She begins every day anew with a large cup of coffee and her Bible in that special corner of the house where she spends time with the Lord.

CPSIA information can be obtained
at www.ICGtesting.com
Printed in the USA
BVHW031624071019
560429BV00004B/393/P